THE KNOW-IT-ALL GUIDE
TO THE TRINITY ALPS

By Wayne F. Moss

GOLDEN STATE PRINTERS, WEAVERVILLE

Mossart
Weaverville, California 96093

LIBRARY OF CONGRESS
CATALOG CARD NO.:   81-80959

  Moss, Wayne F.   1942 —

    The Know-It-All Guide to the Trinity Alps.

  Weaverville, CA : Mossart

  144 p.

8107   810309

ISBN# 0-9606162-0-9

FOR DIXON DOUGLAS JONES
1942-1977
". . . wilder and wilder
I sang
and my loins wrinkled
like the forehead of a sage."
     —I.L.

*The number of people in a wilderness area
diminishes in proportion to the square
of the distance and the cube of
the elevation from the nearest road.*

— PROFESSOR HILDEBRAND

PREFACE

A guidebook is not a substitute for experience and common sense, but this book will give anyone in reasonably good physical condition enough information to hike confidently in the Trinity Alps. It will give the foolhardy just enough rope to hang himself.

People return to the wilderness for a variety of reasons. No one has all the answers. Perhaps there is some danger involved. This is good. Maybe you'll be frightened at night as not everyone can hear what the wilderness has to say. Bigfoot may yet live. Steve Russell once reported hearing excited Chinese voices one night up on Grizzly Creek.

If you need wilderness go to it soon. The Trinity Alps may not be there very much longer. In the near future the fate of the alps will be decided. Not by me or you, but by nameless, faceless, soft-bellied people in Washington D.C. The stakes are high. We all have a lot to lose.

—*WAYNE F. MOSS*

INTRODUCTION

We all have our childhood mountains. The hills we grew up in. Our hills of home. Mine were the Trinity Alps, that tangled mass of granite, trees, water and sky secreted away in the backwaters of Trinity County.

At the time of this writing, the boundaries of the alps are in dispute. There are no natural geographic boundary lines, thus any definition is based on man-made lines. Lumber interests and the Forest Service want the alps to be as small as possible. Other special interest groups would like the wilderness area to cover most of Trinity County.

Twenty-five years ago the boundary lines were simple. They were set forth in a bulletin published by the California Department of Fish and Game in a pamphlet titled "Angler's Guide To Lakes And Streams Of The Trinity Alps." You could pick up a copy at any sporting goods store in Northern California.

It was this document we came to call the "Know-It-All Guide/Map" because of its glaring cartographic errors and deadpan descriptions of often very difficult tasks, "One has to get to the lake as best he can over some rough terrain."

The Know-It-All Map was to be used for information only. To follow it as a reliable map would invite getting lost for sure. But it did set the boundaries of the alps in no uncertain terms. Those limits became our limits and this book covers the alps, the Trinity Alps, as defined by the old Know-It-All.

In the 1950's we would never have left for the alps without our Know-It-All Map. Take this book with you along with a topographic map and use them to either preview or retrospect an area. Memories don't belong in a drawer. Take these along with you.

MAPS

This book does not want to ruin anyone's adventure or spoil the thrill of discovery by being too explicit in directions. The information given coupled with the proper topographic map will keep you close on track.

You will need the following maps to complement the descriptions in this book:

1. Coffee Creek Quadrangle
2. Cecilville Quadrangle
3. Helena Quadrangle
4. Trinity Dam/Lake Quadrangle
   (Minersville)

It is assumed the reader is looking at these maps while using this book for directions as a trail guide. All directions are based on these four maps.

The real sense and feel of the wilderness is beyond guide books and maps. Let your eyes roam over the surface of a topographic map trying to snap the lines into 3-D patterns, the mountains and valleys they represent. The hidden, the remote, the untramelled places are there. Elderberry Duff, Cub Wallow, Bullard's Basin, Willow Creek, Sandy Canyon, French Cove, Devil's Canyon. Places where you can still spend a week and not see a soul.

There are high points in the alps that still hold first ascents for those of the mountaineering ilk that lust after a patch of earth that has never seen a human foot.

The ultimate irony of the alps is that in spite of this area being beaten to death from overuse, there are still places yet to be seen by man.

No item is more important for navigation in strange country than a topographic map. You can order maps and a free index from:

U.S. Geological Survey
Distribution Center
Denver, Colorado 80225

Aerial photos are also available, but cost a bunch more than a map. Use the same Denver address and ask for a photo index (spot index) for $2.50.

Forest maps are usually free at ranger stations in Weaverville, Big Bar and Coffee Creek. They are not much use for detail work on the trail, but will give you the lay of things and the major roads in the area.

You should pick up a wilderness permit from a ranger station prior to entering the alps. At the present time the alps wilderness permit is only a bureaucratic nuisance. Hopefully it will eventually become a management tool to benefit the alps.

Wilderness rangers you may encounter have much to offer. Befriend them. They are on your side in spite of their uniformed appearance.

WEATHER

Season and elevation dictate the climate/weather throughout the alps. Elevations vary from 2000 feet, where it seldom snows, to almost 9000 feet where you can find snow the year round. Most of the time you will be around 6000 feet. Summer days can be very hot with cool nights. 60 degree variations within a 24 hour period are common. I have seen it snow every month in the alps except for July. Summer thundershowers are short, but often violent. Snow is on the ground, lakes frozen, from about November 1st to late April or early May. Some areas are snowbound until nearly July.

JUNE

All but the very highest or north facing country is open. Meadows are damp and soggy. Mosquitoes bothersome. The creeks are high and swollen with passion from the winter. More than one would-be alpsman has cashed in his chips and gone to that great R.E.I. in the sky while attempting to cross a stream. But the waterfalls are everywhere and roaring. There is plenty of drinking water along the trails lined with newly blossomed wildflowers. The mountains are still capped white making a backdrop for the wonderfully unpredictable weather. It might rain every day in June. It could snow. It could be fun.

JULY

These days are more inviting to the alpsman. Days are hot, nights often warm. The streams and lakes have become swimable. There are countless days without a cloud in the sky and wildflowers are going wild at all elevations. Blue and silver are your days, velvet nights allow you to touch the moon. The trails are beginning to wax dusty.

AUGUST

These are the summer days, my friend, that you think will never end. The weather can't hurt you, it is dependable. A thunder shower is a zapping thing of beauty, especially above timberline. Water is getting scarce, but this opens up many new routes walking watercourses, jumping from rock to rock where the creek used to be. Mosquitoes have gone. Days are hot, but the night air has a hint of autumn on its breath. Take a lesson from the leaves.

AFTER SUMMER

For many people this is prime time in the alps. The crowds have gone. Trails and campsites are empty. A touch of color in the trees replaces the faded wildflowers of August. In September the wilderness is wild again. The weather remains stable, but a short rainstorm is common. Even into October there are many warm cloudless days wedged between crisp nights.

NOVEMBER TO APRIL

You're on your own in the mountains in the winter. Consult a book on snow camping and re-read the story of the Donner Party. Leave word of your whereabouts with the Forest Service or Sheriff's Department. Keep your powder dry as any rescue attempt may take several days.

Undoubtedly winter travel in the alps will gain popularity with hikers/skiers. It is an untapped activity. Those folks involved in winter ventures are a breed unto themselves and need no advice from me.

ETIQUETTE

There was a time when we could go to the wilderness and play Lewis and Clark: build fires, carve trees, shoot a few squirrels, and know the wounds would heal. No more. The wilderness is so fragile that a few thoughtless people will spoil it for us all.

Don't dig level spots for your tent.

Don't wash/bathe in water someone may drink.

Don't use soap in any natural water.

No one should know where your toilet is.

Carry out all garbage.
Leave your pets home.
Maintain a low profile.
Maintain a low noise level.
Camp not on the edge of streams, lakes or trails.
Consider not building a fire.
Respect all wildlife.
Don't chop anything down.
Get a Wilderness permit.

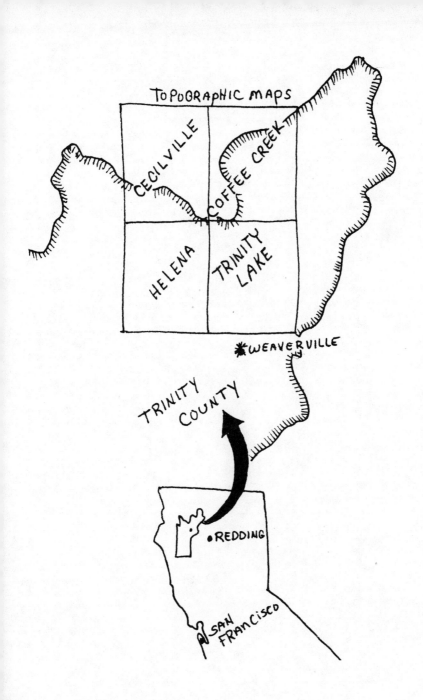

TOPOGRAPHIC MAPS

CECILVILLE

COFFEE CREEK

HELENA

TRINITY LAKE

★WEAVERVILLE

TRINITY COUNTY

•REDDING

SAN FRANCISCO

Lakes of the ALPS

ALPINE LAKE

You wouldn't think that a lake at this elevation would be particularly difficult to get to. Wrong! Once you cross Stuart's Fork, if you can cross Stuart's Fork, it is a pretty stiff climb of almost 3,000 feet vertical to the lake.

Getting across Stuart's Fork can be impossible if the water is high.

However, once you are safely camped at Alpine Lake, an enormous ridge of delight stretches to the north. The prospect of exploring this high, treeless, granite world is enough to ferment the yeast of adventure in the most lethargic alpsman. Alpine is your base camp, or, if you are the travelling type, your first night stop and jump-off point.

Working your way to the north, around the base of peak 8203, will drop you into Smith Lake. This peak, 8203, was years ago unofficially named Trinity Journal Mountain. Fortunately the name didn't stick.

North of Smith is a marvelous ridge of high granite which makes you think of walking upon a gigantic tilted parking lot. At the south end of the parking lot is Sawtooth Peak. Sawtooth Peak should be on every alpsmans' life list.

At the north end of the parking lot is a fantastic aerie where you can perch and overlook Mirror, Emerald and Sapphire Lakes. There is usually ample water from snowmelt.

Alpine Lake is the door to a vertical Wilderness.

11

LAKE ANNA

Prior to the advent of small gas stoves, you built two kinds of fires in the alps; cook fires and man fires.

It was in early October, 1958, when we built that man fire at Lake Anna. A HUGE man fire. All the wood we could muster was piled on at once and the flames seemed to touch the full moon rising like a gigantic hubcap in the east. The four of us sat back about 300 yards from the holocaust and marvelled till way past midnight at how mild the night was for October at 7,000 feet.

That was over 20 years ago. Thanks for gas stoves. I doubt if there is even enough wood left at Anna to build a cook fire.

The lake hangs like a vest pocket on the coat of a very tall man. To get there you come in over the shoulder and drop into the pocket. From East Fork Trailhead it is a pretty steep pull up Long Canyon to Bee Tree Gap. Before you get to the gap, head for the skyline to the south. Stay high (geographically speaking) and you'll hit in above the lake and will only have to drop down once you spot it. Probably only four miles from the car, but plan on four hours of hiking. Steep.

Yes, you could hang left at Bowerman Meadows and reach the lake via the outlet, but it's even steeper than Long Canyon and is best saved as a way to return.

While at Lake Anna you are required to visit Billy-Be-Damned Lake. There are no fish in Billy-Be-Damned.

BEAR LAKE

Foster Lake? Bear Lake? Makes you wonder who is in charge of naming these places.

Whatever its name, you'll find it on the divide between Union Creek and Boulder Creek. Come up either creek or make a loop out of it.

Union Creek is the easier way to do it because the elevation gain is less, plus it is shorter. The trail up Union Creek is more gentle than the Boulder Creek trail and has a few ghosts left over from the Dorleska Mine up in Bullard's Basin.

The last mile below the lake is steep enough to make you breathe hard, but just after crossing Union Creek where the trail starts to climb up to the lake, you'll find a gushing stream that must have a direct line to an ice cave somewhere. So cold, and the last there is until the lake. The old adage of the alps was, "never pass up water."

You might stumble upon Foster/Bear Lake from the Boulder Creek side. This was a lot more fun years back when there was no trail, but now the Forest Service has put in an Interstate type trail over the divide from Lion Lake. In fact, more than one person has been on the way to Lion, failed to look up, and found himself well past Lion and almost over the divide on the way to Bear. There is probably a need for an off ramp for Lion. Why there is a need for a trail in a wilderness is a question we should all ask ourselves.

13

BIG BOULDER LAKE

Mosquitoes! We took our groundcloths and tried to build bug-proof forts with rock walls, but to no avail. Nights were to be dreaded for the want of a bug repellent.

Back in the 1950's it was a long haul from Coffee Creek up to Boulder. Now you can thank the logging industry and drive to within a 35 minute stroll to the lake. Take the Carr Road about one fourth mile south of the Highway #3-Coffee Creek bridge.

I guess a person could still walk in from Goldfield Campground on the old trail, but it would be like visiting a friend dying of a terminal disease. The area has been heavily logged. I should say heavily stripped. Timber product companies have used this area to sharpen their techniques for land rape. Sort of a Guernica for loggers.

Summer of 1958 we were high school kids on the trail to Boulder with home made pack frames loaded heavy with Bernard's dehydrated food. We were the state of the art in alpsmen. This was heavy timber and heavy fantasies. Across the canyon, on Billy's Peak Lookout, was a college girl. Ann Sargent where are you now? We would pant up the trail, out across the brush fields, and collapse in a pile of sweat against our packs as we gazed across the canyon to the lookout. Ann must be sitting cool in a breeze from the window, smelling of all that is female.

Our fantasies fueled us up the seven miles of trail in August of 1958. Big trees. Now you can drive within 35 minutes of the lake.

14

Canyon Creek Boulder Lake. Elevation 5,750 feet; 5 acres; 17 feet deep. Go up the Canyon Creek trail from Dedrick for six miles to Boulder Creek; then another two miles up the Boulder Creek trail to a meadow at the base of the cliff below the lake. From the north side of the meadow a trail goes through dense brush to the bench where the lake is. Stocked with rainbows.

CANYON CREEK BOULDER LAKE

A couple of hundred thousand years ago acres of ice came oozing down Canyon Creek shearing off many of the side canyon entrances. C.C. Boulder Lake is in such a "hanging canyon." Thus the last mile below the lake is a steep climb up onto the shelf wherein lies the lake.

The turnoff is well signed on the Interstate 5 Trail in Canyon Creek. Immediately past the fork in the trail, crossing the creek can be a problem during high water. While you are searching for a crossing point, bear in mind that at least three people have drowned in Canyon Creek just in the past ten years alone. All were in the act of trying to cross the creek.

After crossing the creek, there are quiet meadows, but up ahead you'll see the cliff bands to be scaled. Actually the trail works around to the right to avoid most of the cliffs.

C.C. Boulder is a great mid-summer lake for swimming and sunning. Foot traffic is relatively light. The rocks are warm, flat, granite slabs, perfect for lounging upon. The surface of the water gains warmth as the summer wears on.

My halcyon summer days often find me running from the trailhead to the lake (2 hours), lounging the afternoon away at the lake, running back in the evening (1 hour 20 minutes).

LITTLE BOULDER LAKE

I was sixteen years old when I peeled off my clothes and plunged into the transparent waters of Little Boulder Lake. The first six inches were warm, under that it was close to 32 degrees. Later there was time to lay on warm granite slabs and dream of golden-haired women.

Once, too early in the spring, we tried to follow the old Carrville Trail in, lost the trail and almost ended up down at the bottom of Buckeye Creek.

Southern Pacific and the Forest Service have decided to render this area unfit for wilderness status by building a maze of roads and chopping down all green things over six inches in diameter. They have punched a road to within a 30 minute walk of the lake.

Take the Carr Road, one half mile south of the Coffee Creek-Highway #3 bridge. Follow the road until it ends. The trail takes off at roads end, forks after about a mile (to Big Boulder), stay left and soon you'll drop gently down to Little Boulder.

Recently I sat by Little Boulder during a swirling snowstorm in early December, listened to the throaty song of the wind in the pines, and thought about those kids jumping into the lake those many years ago. My dreams have ceased to be of golden-haired women.

Lower Canyon Creek Lake. Elevation 5,600 feet; 14 acres; 56 feet deep. From Dedrick it is an eight-mile, four-hour trip up Canyon Creek to the lake. All three species, brook, brown and rainbow trout are present, including some large ones. Upper Canyon Creek provides excellent angling for pan-sized trout.

LOWER CANYON CREEK LAKE

This area is the supermarket of the alps. It's all here. Canyon Creek uses its waterfalls, lakes, and magnificent granite to attract more shoppers than any other place in these mountains.

Obviously many people prefer a supermarket such as this. A trip to Canyon Creek Lakes between Memorial Day and Labor Day is strictly a social experience, not a wilderness one.

Like any good supermarket, Canyon Creek crowds are a varied lot. You'll see people packing in gas lanterns, lawn chairs, ice chests (with ice), and chemical toilets. In the evening there are kids chasing about with burning sticks, frisbee games, and rock music from a tape deck.

A friend and I were once routed from our lakeside camp by a spirited game of flashlight tag by a YMCA group from the coast.

Canyon Creek is where the people from the coast come to get warm and dry out. You'll see buses parked at the trailhead. BUSES! Recently, summer of 1980, there was a group of 52 cub scouts and their leaders ensconced at upper meadows. The hills were alive with the sound of screaming.

If the Trinity Alps resemble the Sierra Nevada on a smaller scale, then Canyon Creek resembles Yosemite Valley on a larger one.

To get to the lower lake, simply park at the Canyon Creek Trailhead, which is usually overflowing, and follow the thundering herds up the trail. After the dust settles you'll see the lake, there, between the people.

17

UPPER CANYON CREEK LAKE

In spite of the supermarket feeling of this area, there are some hidden aisles worth exploring in the Canyon Creek drainage.

The upper lake marks the end of about 90% of the crowds. Continue above the upper lake and you'll find a super waterfall, golden trout, and a series of high meadows overflowing with solitude.

From a campsite up there you are in a position to launch an attack upon Mt. Hilton. Check your map and head for the gap to the north of Hilton. Once you get to the gap, and have overcome being overwhelmed by the view down the East Fork of North Fork, get on the west side of the ridge and work your way up to the 8964 foot summit. This is only 38 feet lower than Thompson Peak, highest in the alps. But what a difference! Thompson sees 10-15 people per day during the summer. I doubt if Hilton sees that many over an entire year. And look off to the west. Now that is wilderness down there. No trails, no lakes, no people. Between you and Limestone Ridge is wild country, populated by untouched animals and air.

I've never done it, but a good trip would be to bushwack down the East Fork of North Fork all the way to the road just above Todd Cabin.

Upper Canyon Creek Lake is the 2nd floor of the already crowded supermarket found at the lower lake. Both the upper and lower lake contain huge fish, but they are uncatchable.

BIG CARIBOU LAKE

Le madre grande! This is the big mother. Not only is it the biggest, it is big enough to hold Emerald and Sapphire Lakes and still have room left over for a couple of more lakes. Caribou even has a couple of islands, maybe surf, who knows, maybe its own tide!

Years ago this lake was hard hit by the horsepacking crowd, but that has faded of late. Still, large crowds gather at times, but there is still room for people to spread out. Caribou is a big lake!

It is a short stroll from the lake up to Stuart's Fork Divide. A glance down the other side and you'll see Morris Meadows to the south. Emerald and Sapphire Lakes to the west. The big hunk of mountain to the southwest is Sawtooth Peak (8886 feet high in the sky). Zigzagging down into Stuart's Fork is the trail known locally as KT-87. Someone counted 87 kick-turns, or switchbacks, from the divide down to Portuguese Camp. I think they underestimated the number.

The Caribou Basin is a fairly easy eight miles from the trailhead at Big Flat now that a new trail skirts around the mountain. The old trail went right up over Caribou Mountain — a little shorter, but a real gut-buster.

Pick a campsite on the west side of the lake and be rewarded with alpenglow on Caribou Mountain in the evening, and fantastic reflections of the moon on the water as it rises over the shoulder of the mountain.

Little Caribou Lake. Elevation 7,150 feet; 3 acres; 16 feet deep. This lake, which is not situated in the Caribou Basin, is a two-hour ride from Big Flat, the last mile more suited to mule than horse travel. Contains brook trout.

LITTLE CARIBOU LAKE

When the good Lord made the alps he must have had a lake left over and no place to put it. There was a time when people at least *saw* Little Caribou as they ascended the old, gut-busting ridge trail to Big Caribou. Now, the new trail gives no hint that up at the head of Conrad Gulch is a nice little lake.

Follow the new trail until you're pretty sure you're in Conrad Gulch. Check your map. Up above the trail will be slabs of white granite. It isn't too difficult to pick and bounce up the granite to the lake. Should you find that some thoughtless person has left rock ducks to mark the way, kindly destroy them. The persons coming after you will have the wilderness enjoyment of route-finding you were denied by the duck builder.

A stay at Little Caribou will please the fisherman, sunbather, reader, and seeker of nothing to do. It is a lot like the small town bypassed by the new interstate highway. It makes a nice destination for a day hike from Big Flat.

Anytime someone tells you they have been to *every* lake in the alps, hit'em with Little Caribou. Chances are they'll have to lie to say they've been there.

Yup, the Lord just had one too many lakes on his hands.

Lower Caribou Lake. Elevation 6,500 feet; 22 acres; 83 feet deep. Located at the lower end of the Caribou Basin. A beautiful deep lake surrounded by high, steep mountains and sheer granite cliffs. Has rainbow and brook trout, some of large size.

LOWER CARIBOU LAKE

Caribou country is Steele country — Ethel Steele Pettis. Her family has dominated this area for over 100 years. It was Ethel's great-grandfather, James Abrams, who built a cabin at Big Flat in 1850. They got into the horsepacking business early and have been up and down the mountains of this part of the alps ever since.

It was the Steeles that helped pack fish to the Caribou Basin back in the 1930's.

Ethel Steele was way ahead of women's lib and the ERA. She was doing it and doing it herself for over 41 years. She was training young women in the horsepacking game before anyone figured it might be contrary to traditional sex roles.

Ethel once said, "Really living is sleeping out in the wilderness under the stars."

"I've never been lost and I've never lost a guest."

When I hike into Lower Caribou Lake, I can't help but wonder why I didn't meet up with Ethel Steele 20 years ago when we both could have profited from a relationship between us and the alps.

Lower Caribou can be a sanctuary if you set your camp over on the far north side, opposite where the trail passes. The lake is big enough to make a good buffer from the sometimes crowd of people passing on their way to Big Caribou. Besides, over there, your back door opens out onto a huge hunk of wilderness.

MIDDLE CARIBOU

A typical reaction to Middle Caribou is, "What! Where's the lake?"

But, sure enough, there it is tucked under the base of a nice bunch of granite, a little waterfall at the outlet, with someone camped on the shoreline.

You can see the bait-sized brook trout with white tipped fins cruising the clear water. If you could comprehend and understand all that is contained within this one half acre lake, the secrets of the alps would be yours. A day by Middle Caribou must enrich your life, saturate every part of your body with the beauty of forever.

Watch the expressions that appear across the lake. A passing cloud, a flash of sun, even the dab of a dragonfly touching the surface. Maybe this is what John Muir had in mind when describing lakes that lie nestled in glacier wombs.

"How boundless the day seems as we revel in the storm-beaten sky gardens amid so vast a congregation of onlooking mountains." —J.M.

Old John never made it to Middle Caribou, but it's just as well. In the alps you can be your own John Muir. Write your own book! Sing your own songs.

Carters Little Mud Lake. Area—1 acre. Maximum depth—8 feet. Elevation—6,300 feet. This small lake can be reached by taking the trail from Caribou Basin to the Middle Fork of South Fork of Salmon River and working up to the lake from that trail. It is doubtful that this lake would sustain a trout population and at present no plans have been made to plant it.

CARTERS LITTLE MUD LAKE

Here is an example of the humor to be found in the original Know-It-All Guide. Carter's Little Mud Lake. Not many people are laughing. Not even the ones fortunate enough to find it. Not many have found it. Even fewer people want to.

Carter is an old pioneer name in these mountains. Obviously some wag found the most obscure puddle and, in jest, bestowed upon it the revered Carter name.

O.K., where is it? Not named on the topographic map, but follow the Middle Fork of Little South Fork to the source. That small blue circle marks the frog-pond called Carter's Little Mud Lake. Does the name make you think of pills too?

This is fine, wild country. No trails. Just you and your wits on a north flowing stream. Perhaps if you were to spend the night here you'd be able to see a glow in the sky from the campfires over the ridge at Big Caribou.

The easiest way to get here is over the ridge from Big Caribou. Aim directly for the low spot directly to the west. Once in this gap, it is straight down to the lake.

You could come in on the trail up out of the main South Fork. When you hit the outlet, follow it to the lake.

Then there is that montane chaparral slope to the north of Emerald Lake, Sawtooth Ridge. It could be done, but rough!

Only a highly motivated alpsman with private reasons will visit Carter's Little Mud.

23

Deer Lake. Elevation 7,150 feet; 4.5 acres; 19 feet deep. Accessible by trail up Stuart Fork and thence up Deer Creek, up the Stoney Creek Ridge trail from Stuart Fork, or by way of Long Canyon. Brook trout to 10 inches were common in 1966. Other lakes nearby.

DEER LAKE

If you come into Deer Lake before mid-July you'll be able to use the Gratton Flat Gang's "slide for life." From Deer Creek Pass it is possible to glissade 300-400 feet down to the lake. Five minutes down, an hour to hike back out.

We were here once when only a thin sliver of the lake was unfrozen. The entire lake was ice covered except for a 15 foot strip along an edge. Putting salmon eggs on hooks and casting out onto the ice, we'd pull in line until the bait fell off the ice into the lake. WHAM! Everytime a fish. Two guys caught and released about 50 fish in an hour.

Firewood is nonexistent at the lake. There is only one tree available for shade, so if you are the first one there, the only campsite is yours.

The enormous mountain massif of beautiful gray granite to the east of you has no name. 8207 feet high, it is often mistaken for Seven-up Peak. Seven-Up is lower and further to the north.

To the west, towering over the lake, is Siligo Peak (8162 ft.)

The practical way to reach Deer Lake is to come up Long Canyon from the East Fork Trailhead, cross Siligo Meadows to Deer Creek Pass, and drop down to the lake.

But if you love long walks, come up Deer Creek from Morris Meadows on Stuart's Fork. It'll take you all day.

24

DIAMOND LAKE

Diamond Lake is a place to dream. To the west the arena of the alps provides the stuff dreams are composed of. A place to dine on clouds. You can dine on clouds and know you are growing older by the way the moon makes lines on your face with no lines. But clouds don't taste all that bad when the dining room is Diamond Lake.

The warm runny days of summer seem to never end. The sun hangs forever in the west and the temptation to look at it has to be resisted.

In the late 1950's we killed a lot of fish in Diamond. When we tired of fishing, we stripped off and swam in water more fit for trout than humans. We were going to live forever as we stretched out on the grass to dry in the sun. Once Dixon Jones cranked up our fantasies with the story that a whole troop of girl scouts once came to this very lake and swam in their underwear. Our fertile adolescent minds fed on that thought for hours.

But Diamond Lake is not forever. Love it while you are there, eat a few clouds. If it's a warm day, take a dip. Stay as long as you can. I may be wrong about the whole thing.

Big East Fork Lake. Elevation 5,850 feet; 2 acres; 11 feet deep. Since this small lake is out of the way it is seldom visited. Has both brook and rainbow trout. From Dedrick on Canyon Creek a trail follows up Big East Fork of Canyon Creek to the lake.

BIG EAST FORK LAKE

The trail to Big East Fork starts at Buck's Ranch. There are several ways to get to Buck's Ranch, but they are changing all the time. Roads for mining claims and timber sales come and go. You can start walking from Dedrick, the Maple Mine, or at any point along the maze of roads where your vehicle can go no farther.

Once past Buck's Ranch, it is a very steep walk. The last mile or so across a brush field reaches skin-scalding temperature on a summer afternoon.

A good alternative is to get dropped off at the East Weaver Lake Trailhead on the Weaver Bally Road and cross over to the Rush Creek Lakes. From the lower Rush Creek Lake, it is a short ways down the trail to a point near the low gap west of Peak 6844. From this gap it is less than 30 minutes to contour around to Big East Fork Lake. Then you can exit *down* to the road at Dedrick.

Fishing for those little brook trout is always good at this lake. However, the real charm of this place is that it is de facto wilderness. Because of the remote location and lack of access, it will probably remain wilderness even without federal protection.

Walk up on the ridge to the west: look down into Van Matre Creek. Now there's some wilderness where hopefully a road will never be built.

Echo Lake. Elevation 7,250 feet; 2.5 acres; 17 feet deep. The best route is up the Stoney Creek Ridge trail, through Stonewall Pass and past Van Matre Meadows. Just below Little Stonewall pass, a dim trail goes in a southerly direction past a small pond to the lake. Stocked with brook trout.

ECHO LAKE

The geologists probably have a name for it, but I call it a balcony lake. You can sit on the bank of Echo Lake, as if in a balcony, and dangle your feet and thoughts out over Deep Creek and that giant emptiness over Stuart's Fork. The best show from this balcony starts at sundown each evening.

But a moondown can be just as rewarding. I remember a night there years ago when the moon was full—one of those huge moons at high altitude that makes it impossible to sleep because of the brightness. And who knows what primeval stirrings it causes in the heart of an alpsman.

It was a huge hubcap of a moon. The old saying of being able to read by the moon was easy to prove that night. There are few trees for shade from such a moon. When it finally set that night at Echo, we all felt relief, turned back into our kapok bags and tried to sleep until noon.

The classic approach to this lake is through Stonewall Pass from Red Mountain Meadows, but that trailhead is hard to find since they have logged the hell out of Granite Peak and destroyed the lower part of the trail.

You'd be safer coming over from Siligo Meadows via Little Stonewall Pass.

But if you are adventurous, come up Stoney Ridge and explore the Red Mountain, Middle Peak, and Granite Peak massif on the way.

27

LAKE ELEANOR

Eleanor, queen of the Alps. But the queen has been despoiled. The devil's cohort, Southern Pacific, has seen fit to punch roads and take logs within an axe throw of the lake.

Eleanor was always open first in the spring, thus it was the first shakedown trip of the season. As went Eleanor, so went the rest of the summer.

It was three miles from Gratton Flat back in the old days. Now it is a ten minute walk from a nearby logging road. In case you get lonely for civilization, Southern Pacific has built a road, an ugly scar, across the ridge above the lake. Even a moron can be an engineer. They took the trees and left a road. A double slap in the face to all of us who loved to listen to the frogs croak in the evening by Lake Eleanor.

In 1958 we never took a tent. Just laid out under the stars there by the inlet. Crawling into a tent in the alps is akin to taking a shower with your socks on.

We woke up one morning to see a huge owl peering down on us from a nearby snag. Carefully ol' Ron rolled over in his bag, drew a bead with his .22, and squeezed the trigger. He missed a mile. The owl jumped two.

Later, flat on our backs floating on air mattresses, we caught 26 brook trout.

Ell Lake. Elevation 6,530 feet; 2 acres; 29 feet deep. From Upper Canyon Creek Lake outlet a dim trail goes to the lake; a good hour and a half climb. Brook trout do very well in this "L" shaped lake.

ELL LAKE

Ell Lake occupies a narrow groove in a side canyon of Canyon Creek at the base of Sawtooth Peak's north face. The music of geologic orchestra is here if we could only develop an ear for it. The music is there, but it is being played on a record turning on a turntable that rotates once every 10,000 years.

High above the lake the north face of Sawtooth is always in a blue haze of shadowed granite. Often the sun never shines on this side of the mountain.

A campsite at Ell will spare you the crowds that clamor back down at the Canyon Creek Lakes. It will also afford you a base camp for visits up on the divide for vistas into Stuart's Fork.

You can follow the ridge to the north of the lake and wonder what of the rain that falls here. In the space of a few feet it either gets to flow free to the sea, down Canyon Creek, or is shunted off to Southern California via tunnels and dams of the Central Valley Project. Which way would you rather flow?

Your walk along the ridge can lead you to Mirror Lake or Kalmia in a relatively short time.

An assault of Sawtooth Peak from this area would be a challenge worthy of any would-be alpsman.

EMERALD LAKE

James W. Bartlett, when he footnoted *Cox's Annals of Trinity County,* put it thusly:

"The tribute paid to the wilderness and stupendous scenery of the mountains among which the stream known as Stewart's Fork rises and wends its way into the Trinity River is well merited. The hills and peaks are mainly of granite: scattered through them are a number of beautiful lakes, some of these being near the tops of the mountains: at some points are to be found perpetual snows: the streams are well stocked with mountain trout: the woods are inhabited by bear, black and brown, by deer, foxes, coyotes, and at some places the mountain lion."

There are people that consider a trip to Emerald Lake the only trip worthy of being called a trip in the alps. To them, this is the alps.

They have a point. The lake is large, geographically centered, on the largest stream, at the end of the longest hike, and has a name denoting the jewel it is.

Unfortunately the place attracts a crowd all summer long. Better you should push on to Sapphire Lake or beyond.

The remnants of the dam on the outlet were used at the turn of the century to control the water level for downstream mining operations.

30

FORBIDDEN LAKE

Now how could anyone resist a name like *Forbidden?* The name is a lure to adventure, romance, forbidden things.

What you'll find is a pretty slip of a lake tucked in a thin crease in the mountain above Canyon Creek Boulder Lake.

There are campsites that offer an eagle's view of upper Canyon Creek, or are intimate against the lake. The sun comes up about noon and goes down at 2:00 p.m. so narrow is the canyon.

This is a fine base camp on the edge of wilderness for the advanced alpsman only. The country to the west is trackless. Up the draw above the lake notice the two low gaps. Get up into the right gap and you'll have at your feet the headwaters of the East Fork of North Fork. This is untravelled, untramelled, unbelievable wilderness. Waterfalls, granite cliffs, miles to wander in if you're brave enough. There are no trails down there.

The left hand gap will put you in touch with equally untouched country, the East Branch of the East Fork of North Fork. What a mouthful. The terrain is as complex as the name.

You could head off downstream and wind up the trail at McClaron Mine. Trailhead is on down at the fork with the East Fork above Todd Cabin.

Between McClaron Mine and Todd Cabin the main hazards are rattlesnakes and marijuana farms.

Found Lake. Area—2½ acres. Maximum depth—9 feet. Elevation—6,800 feet. This lake is situated above Lost Lake, which is above Big Boulder Lake. It is three hours to Big Boulder Lake and then another hour up to Found Lake. It was planted with eastern brook trout in 1952, but is a "borderline" water: only time will tell if it will support a population of fish.

FOUND LAKE

Found Lake is the finale of Boulder Creek. The name "lake" may be a misnomer for the frog pond you're going to find at the end of a 45 minute hike up from Big Boulder Lake.

There is no trail, but none is needed because all you do is follow the stream or drainage, stream bed after mid-summer, from Big Boulder, to Lost Lake, to Found.

The late afternoon sun in 1958 was backlighting the airborne pine pollen that drifted about the forest. I was young enough to be able to linger that summer above Found Lake for no reason. I sat for hours on the granite boulders above Cub Wallow watching a hawk climb the shadows up out of the canyon. The dark texture of trees beyond the hawk, covering the faraway ridge, was really the hair on my leg, only the hair on my leg wasn't my leg, it was the faraway ridge, and it wasn't the forest or mountains, but my body. People climb the shadows looking for places to camp in my brain, leaving their garbage in my bloodstream digging a latrine near my heart.

Fortunately no one stays for long. Found Lake is only open four or five months of the year.

Gibson Lake. Area—¼ acre. ˙ Maximum depth—7 feet. Elevation—6,000 feet. Gibson Lake is a small body of water that can be reached by taking the Swift and Granite Creek trails to the lower end of Gibson Meadow and then making one's way south from the lower end of the meadow. This is another lake whose ability to support fish is questionable. The first fish, eastern brook trout, were scheduled to be planted in this lake in 1953.

GIBSON LAKE

Gibson is one of the hide-and-go-seek lakes. It's out there hidden and your task is to find it if you want to play the game.

Start by finding your way to Gibson Meadows. This is actually downstream from the area marked "Gibson Meadows" on the topographic map. Across the creek from the trail is an open patch of hillside. Find the open patch and then find the outlet stream. This stream ends in a small boggy pond that I presume is Gibson Lake.

However, if you contour around to the east, there is a lake of small proportions that could be Gibson too. Take your pick. It isn't important.

The value of Gibson Lake is it offers an alternative to an otherwise overused area. Granite Creek and Granite Lake are trampled to death all summer long. But yet just a few minutes from this interalps freeway is a personal, one-person lake almost totally ignored.

But there may be some truth in the argument that ¼ acre of seven foot deep water does not a lake make.

Whatever your reason for going to Gibson Lake, you'll have to look for it. No trail. A worthy test of your routefinding skills.

Granite Lake. Area—18 acres. Maximum depth—64 feet. Elevation—7,300 feet. It is four miles up the Swift Creek trail to Granite Creek, and then another three miles up the Granite Creek trail to Granite Lake. Granite Lake is one of possibly two lakes in the Siskiyou-Trinity Area to contain Lahontan cutthroat trout. The predominate fish in this water, though, are brown trout and some are reported "big enough to tow a raft around." Some fair-sized rainbows are also present.

GRANITE LAKE

If Canyon Creek is the supermarket of the alps, Granite Lake is the parking lot. There are times when all the campsites at the lake are filled with old, beat-up '47 Pontiacs disguised as backpackers.

People who have heard of the alps expect spectacular scenery. Especially those who got their info from *Sunset* magazine. Granite Lake fills the bill, and as a result, people fill the scenery. Yet by picking carefully the time and season you can avoid the crowds. Try anytime before Memorial Day if the winter has been mild, or after Labor Day.

This is azalea heaven from the end of June into July. The pungent smell, sweet and thick in the air, provides the incentive to wander further and further up the trail.

The trail is but five miles in length from car to lakeside. During the three to four hours required to walk it, you will see waterfalls, luxuriant meadows, deep woods, sky scratching peaks. It's all here. Just like it said in *Sunset*.

Only have a day? You can run (jog) into this lake in a little over an hour, spend the day, and allow 45 minutes in the evening to return.

Don't miss the view from the rock promontory just across the outlet on the east side of the lake. This is a place to sun, swim, and eye-climb Gibson Peak (8400 ft.). Gibson rears up so suddenly on the far side you could get whiplash looking too quickly.

GRIZZLY LAKE

And where is Nirvana in the alps? When all desire for existence is extinquished and your soul becomes one with the Creator, open your eyes and you'll be at Grizzly Lake. Unfortunately I'm afraid you'll find Nirvana is a rather crowded place.

Grizzly became accessible when the route from China Creek over by Cecilville was developed. Prior to that time it was a long, delicious, trek of 18 miles from Hobo Gulch. Some folks still make that hike from Hobo, but they are few. The hordes of people thunder in over the ridge from China Creek. There is an apocrythal story of Dixon Jones making it in three and one half hours from trailhead to lake. He probably did.

But even with the crowds, doing Grizzly is worth it. The waterfall at the outlet provides the appropriate background for watching the sunset roar golden and orange off to the west over the tumbled mass of hills where surely Bigfoot sleeps.

Thompson Peak broods and sulks behind a never melting snowbank.

If you should die after visiting Grizzly Lake, all is well, you've already seen the best the alps can offer. You couldn't pick a better place to take your last trip. From Grizzly Meadows to the lake there is a chance for testing your skills at routefinding. Please destroy any rock ducks so as not to deprive those who follow the experience someone denied you.

Horseshoe Lake. Elevation 6,850 feet; 6 acres; 22 feet deep. Situated at the head of Swift Creek, it is 14.5 miles by trail from the end of the road. Brook trout are abundant and doing very well.

HORSESHOE LAKE

Horseshoe Lake is a nifty little lake tucked away under the watchful eye of Tri-Forest Peak at the headwaters of Swift Creek. The sun goes down early, but jumps up early, in the east, like a red rubber ball.

The route up Swift Creek is a piece of cake. Only the last mile or so involves any sudden elevation gain.

On the way from the Swift Creek trailhead the landmarks pass easily; Granite Creek where probably 80% of the traffic turns off, Steer Creek (to be waded in early season), Parker Creek with bomb proof bridge, the old cabin at Parker Meadow, and finally the long sloping beauty of Mumford Meadow. A campsite in Mumford allows a good base to wander this gentle country. Wander up to Mumford *Basin* where the feeling of the alps of 100 years ago prevails. A day hike from here over into Black's Basin, Long Cabin, and then down Bear Basin provides a wilderness experience so exquisite you'll swear it's illegal.

But if you push on to Horseshoe, the granite is white and beautiful. There's plenty of firewood should you feel the urge for a man fire.

From a lakeside camp, be sure and get up on Tri-Forest Peak.

Of course you can come in to Horseshoe via Kidd Creek over by Big Flat. It's like entering a huge house from the back door. You miss all the good stuff. It is shorter and steeper, but could be used to complete a loop trip. Or to save time if you happen to be in a rush because you're double parked somewhere.

Josephine Lake. Elevation 5,800 feet; 17 acres; 47 feet deep. Josephine Lake is located near the headwaters of the South Fork of the Salmon River. Being privately owned it is *not* stocked by the Department of Fish and Game.

JOSEPHINE LAKE

It's a shame, but this lake somehow has ended up in private ownership. Deplorable as this is in the eyes of wilderness lovers, the lake is not available to the public until perhaps a smart enough lawyer comes along and argues it back into the alps.

If someone can own a lake in the alps, they might as well own the clouds, the rain, the thunder of a summer storm.

Josephine is like a fjord fitted into a tight granite slot adjacent to Caribou Mountain. High walls of rock on either side keep the sunshine hours to a minimum and may bring out latent claustrophobia in some people.

Drive to the end of Coffee Creek Road. If you come to a locked gate, that's it. Park and start walking. If you are overnighting, leave your car back at Big Flat Campground.

If the gate is open, drive to Carter's Resort and ask for permission to leave your car there. It is private property, but don't be intimidated. They only own a very small chunk of the canyon (section 31) and can't prevent you from free travel through the area. The south end of the lake is public land. In spite of what anyone at Carter's might say, you can camp there (at the south end of Josephine).

Kalmia Lake. Elevation 7,500 feet; 1 acre; 13 feet deep. Named for the "mountain laurel" that grows along its shore. Situated north of Upper Canyon Creek Lake near the top of the mountain. Hike up towards Ell Lake, then through the timber to the gap between Canyon Creek and Stuart Fork then work around in a westerly direction on the Canyon Creek side to the lake. Stocked with brook trout.

KALMIA LAKE

This pristine niche would have been a magnificent ringside seat during the late Jurassic ice flow that came crunching and grinding past Kalmia Lake at the rate of a few inches per year.

The western edge of the lake is still a magnificent ringside seat. The river of ice is gone, but the huge U-shaped valley of Canyon Creek pluton is there stretching off to the south, a reminder and vivid example of the stunning forces that shaped this part of the alps.

Kalmia Lake will have ice on the surface until July.

Being almost on the ridge top gives the Kalmia camper outstanding views in all directions. A short walk to the east opens the upper Stuart's Fork drainage to feast eyes upon. Mirror Lake is only a couple of stone throws away. Emerald and Sapphire nestle like jewels in a granite setting.

To the west is a head-on look at Thompson and Wedding Cake Peaks. At this distance they are over-powering in size. Let your eyes scale them.

To reach Kalmia, go up to Ell Lake, make for the low gap on the divide and then contour north to the lake.

LANDERS LAKE

Red. Red is the color of the rocks that tumbled down off the mountain to surround Landers Lake. When you see that mountain, you'll know what its name is.

Landers Lake is right up close to the top of things — kind of a mountain top lake where a short walk in several directions results in long views.

Over to the north you can prop up against a rock and let your eyes hike off down Union Creek and over to Battle Mountain.

Or, a little exertion and you'll be up on Red Rock Mountain, to the west, watching dangling skirts of a thunderstorm scrape the peaks of the Marble Mountains far and away to the north. Those dark valleys seem to swallow, in great gulps, the jags of lightning. Dead ahead of you is Caribou Mountain. Were there ever Caribou in those mountains?

Still to the north, below you from left to right, is a valley that looks as if a giant finger pushed through the primeval clay of the alps leaving the upper reaches of the South Fork of the Salmon River. But, abruptly, it heads due west. Stream piracy the geologists call it.

Coffee Creek was beheaded at Big Flat by glaciation. The stream from melting ice chose to go west. Coffee Creek starts less than a mile away and flows east.

There is much to be learned from sitting on mountain tops.

Lilypad Lake. Area—2 acres. Maximum depth—8 feet. Elevation—6,300 feet. This lake is at the head of Poison Canyon, a tributary of the North Fork of Swift Creek. It can be reached by any of five routes. There are two trails up the North Fork, one up Hatchet Creek (north of Trinity Center), one from the head of Big Boulder Creek, and one from the head of Parker Creek. The best fishing in this lake is in early summer, since later the surface becomes completely covered with lily pads, making it nearly impossible to fish. Eastern brook trout are plentiful and some are of fair size.

LILYPAD LAKE

Yes, there are a lot of lilypads in this lake late in the summer. Best time, unless you plan to study lilypads, is about mid-June until early in July.

You can come in from the Lake Eleanor Road via Shimmy Lake, or up the trail in Poison Canyon. I suppose a few people make their way over from the Boulder country, too, since one autumn we came upon a deer hunter with a broken leg. He had wandered over from Big Boulder Lake. We helped him down Poison Canyon and on into town.

Poison Canyon got its name from the sheepmen that lost a lot of sheep in the canyon when they ate black laurel. My youngest daughter was stung by yellowjackets here one afternoon. Luckily she didn't eat any black laurel.

Either route you choose to the lake will take you close to Ycatapom Peak. Up Poison Canyon you can admire the staggering north face. Coming over from Shimmy Lake, you'll pass close enough to the summit to wander over and take a heart-stopping look down the north face.

Ycatapom is an Indian word that means the mountain that leans to the north.

LION LAKE

Don't be a fool and hike into Lion Lake from Goldfield Campground. Only people on horseback use that trail.

Drive to the trailhead at the end of the Carr Road. Hike into Big Boulder Lake and then drop down the trail (north) about a mile. Find the trail to your left that contours around into Boulder Creek. If you can't find it, contour anyway. You can't miss Boulder Creek. Once you hit the creek, head upstream until you hit the outlet stream of the lake coming in from your right. Follow the outlet up past a couple of ponds until Lion Lake hoves into view.

There is a lot of white granite and blue sky here. A short jaunt up over the low gap beyond the lake will put you on Bear/Foster Lake.

While at Lion Lake, you would be remiss not to explore the upper reaches of Boulder Creek. You'll find small but fiesty trout to catch in the stream for a ways. Follow it far enough and you'll be in another of those secret places of the alps — solitude guaranteed. The place is called Cub Wallow. The experience is lonesome. The wild animals match the small meadow at the very headwall of the canyon. Both wild.

Lost Lake. Area—1¾ acres. Maximum depth—15 feet. Elevation—6,700 feet. It is a 15-minute climb (no trail) up to this lake from Big Boulder Lake. Eastern brook trout are plentiful.

LOST LAKE

On the topographic map this is called Tapie Lake. Tapie or Lost is not the problem. Calling it a lake is. There are a number of ponds in the alps of this caliber, but they were not fortunate enough to receive a name. Yet here sits this one with two.

Work your way up through the rock outcroppings above Big Boulder Lake. The lake is not hard to find.

After you've had your fill of Lost Lake, there'll be plenty of time left over to do a little scrambling on the unnamed peak to the south. Once up on top, give yourself a nice geography lesson. Way over across Poison Canyon is Ycatapom Peak. Ycatapom is an Indian name which means whatever an Indian wants it to mean. "Mountain that leans to the north" is one given meaning.

Straight to the north you can study the route followed by the old trail/jeep road into Boulder country.

Off to the west you can peek into Cub Wallow.

Way to the north is Mt. Shasta. While at shorter range is Billy's Peak. No, the lookout on top is no longer manned (womanned; see entry under Big Boulder Lake).

After the time you've spent on this unnamed peak, you'll feel that your trip to Lost Lake was not lost after all.

LUELLA LAKE

I was sure anxious to see this lake when just a kid. There was a restaurant in Weaverville called Luella's and it always flashed in my mind when I saw the name on the map. Was there a connection? Would Luella Lake resemble Luella's Cafe? When I finally got there, I could find no resemblance, but then things change, people change, cafes change.

Up above Deer Creek Meadows Luella squats, waiting. People rarely stay. Either they are passing by on the way to Diamond Lake, or heading down to the meadows. I have never personally met anyone who has actually camped at this lake. Maybe it's the Luella Cafe complex. No one camps on cafes either. A change of name might change Luella Lake's life.

Like other lakes in this area, the direct approach is from East Fork Trailhead, up Long Canyon, across Siligo Meadows, and then loop either left or right around Siligo Peak to the lake.

The other approach is from Morris Meadow and up Deer Creek — a long, long way from the trailhead on Stuart's Fork at Bridge Camp.

You could come over from Granite Lake through the low gap across the canyon from Luella to the east. Lots of ways to get to Luella. You might give the old girl a surprise and camp there, too.

43

MILL CREEK LAKE

Lois Lake (Mill Creek Lake) is the most *looked* at Lake in the alps. The usual practice is to hike up from Grizzly Lake, look down at Lois, and then proceed on.

Well, I walked down to it one August day because I had to touch it. All my life this two and one half acres had been perceived as the most difficult, inaccessible lake in the alps. That's what the old Know-It-All Guide said. Savor the thought. Most inaccessible.

It fired my imagination for years. Who can rest easy when they haven't yet been to the most inaccessible lake in the alps. No matter how tough other hikes in the alps may have been, there was one tougher, Lois Lake.

Sometimes I'd wake up in the night and wonder what it was like up there at that moment. On snowy days, while walking around town, I'd think of what it must be like snowed in at Lois Lake. A white lonesome world.

It probably was the most inaccessible back in the days when you had to start walking at Hobo Gulch Trailhead. Then it was a long, long way up North Fork and Grizzly Creek to Lois. Now, you can come in from Cecilville via China Spring. Figure five hours to Grizzly Lake and then another hour up to Lois and it's not a whole lot harder than many other alps trips.

Should the crowds at Grizzly get on your nerves, Lois is a good escape. It faces west to guarantee spine tingling sunsets.

If you go to Lois, you'd be crazy not to loop on up to Thompson Peak, highest in the alps.

44

Mirror Lake.   Area—14 acres.   Maximum depth—25 feet.   Elevation—7,400 feet.   Seventeen miles of trail up the Stuart Fork brings one to the lower end of Sapphire Lake, from where a foot trail leads to the upper end of Sapphire. From there it is necessary to climb up to Mirror Lake. It takes nearly one and three-quarter hours of foot work. Both brookies and rainbow are found here; the rainbows are reported to reach greater than average size.

MIRROR LAKE

Reflect on the name of this lake for a moment. What would you expect of a lake with the name of Mirror?

This lake is at the very heart of the alps. No, not geographically, but spiritually. You can't go much further up Stuart's Fork than Mirror Lake. You can't go deeper into the alps than Mirror. Just over the ridge is Canyon Creek, or Grizzly Lake, or South Fork Lake. Caribou Basin is not far. Thompson Peak and Sawtooth Peak punch the nearby sky. Nope, you can't get much deeper into the alps. You would expect a lake in this location to Mirror the alps. It does. After a 17 mile walk up Stuart's Fork, you have arrived at the heart of it all.

Those snow banks up above never melt. The peak you have to crank your head all the way back to look at is so wild and free that it has no name. It is only 36 feet shorter than Thompson Peak and two feet higher than Hilton, making it the second highest peak in the alps. Ironically, at 8966 feet, it remains nameless and unknown.

Mirror Lake campsites put the alpsman in the throne room of the mountain kings. Nobody can bother you up here in this granite vault.

Of late, more and more people have discovered that it is a bit shorter, albeit rougher, to approach Mirror from Canyon Creek via Ell Lake. I have done this route, in and back, in one day. So has Dick Everest. It makes for a very long day.

MORAINE LAKE

No one would ever go to Moraine Lake except that it is a close neighbor of Little South Fork Lake and you can't miss it on your way to L.S.F.L.. It may have been a mistake to name it, but someone did, so we have to deal with it as a legitimate alps lake.

Rivers, creeks, and streams that run in a northward direction generate a mystery of their own. What a north face is to a mountain climber, a north flowing stream is to an alpsman.

When you're on a north flowing stream the country seems foreign. It leads away from the places familiar. The sun shines less, it rains and snows more, and the nights last longer at a northside lake like Moraine.

The potential for adventure increases as we push onto north faces.

To reach Moraine, heed the instructions outlined under Little South Fork Lake elsewhere in this book.

Moraine offers a place to test this equation:

"The number of people in a Wilderness area diminishes in proportion to the square of the distance and the cube of the elevation from the nearest road."—Professor Hildebrand

MORRIS LAKE

There is only one way to go to Morris Lake, up Canyon Creek. The old Know-It-All Guide started the rumor about going up Bear Gulch from Morris Meadows. Bull! More than one person has cussed himself all the way home for taking that advice.

First of all, Morris Meadows is ten miles from the trailhead, then it is a three hour bushwack and rattlesnake stomp to the lake.

On the other hand, you could walk for an hour and a half up Canyon Creek, hang a right turn at the first major gulch past the meadows, and you'll be at Morris Lake hours before those dopes down in Bear Gulch doing hand-to-hand combat with the rattlesnakes.

Actually you shouldn't go exactly up the gulch out of Canyon Creek. Stay on the south edge (right side) of the ridge and head for the big boulder field that leads to the flat, but tilted, granite slabs. Contour gradually to your left and gain enough altitude to hit the low gap on the divide.

Morris is a nice little penthouse above Smith Lake. Can't say much about the fishing, but the rumor has it there are golden trout in there.

The view of the south side of Sawtooth Peak is uncluttered. As you gaze upwards, ask yourself if it is possible that someone has climbed that cliff, or better still, ask yourself if anyone ever will.

From Morris, you can take the tourist route to Sawtooth's summit by circling around to the east, then up.

MUD LAKE

If the alps have a forgotten closet way back in the rear of the house somewhere, this is it. Mud Lake. Mud Lake by any other name would still be a mud lake. It is not very high on anyone's priority list of must-see lakes.

I first came across it while on the way to bigger and better (so I thought) Lion Lake. We had lost the trail coming over from Big Boulder and were fighting our way cross country to Lion when we stumbled upon Mud Lake.

So what the heck, said I. A fishing lure cast casually among the lilypads brought everyone to their feet instantly. It appeared the lake was full of Pihranna fish so vicious was the attack on the lure. A fish, though hooked, would be assaulted by other fish as they tried to get the same lure. It was crazy. Sometimes a fish would get free, but another one would grab it right up. We stayed and caught fish until our arms and wrists gave out from fatigue.

On up to Lion we went where between four of us we caught one fish!

On the topographic map this lake is called Conway. Frederick Edmond Conway was an early miner on Swift Creek, born 1856.

Neither Conway nor Mud is a very descriptive name for this lilypad pond.

48

PAPOOSE LAKE

Papoose Lake is what Grizzly Lake used to be like 20 years ago — wild, isolated, a chance to see a bear up close and personal.

Turn off the interstate highway that runs up North Fork. Take the Rattlesnake exit and step back in time. Issac Cox reports a store, butcher shop, and blacksmith shop along with a population of 60 men, no women, in 1856. You can still see all the rocks they moved for several miles as you walk up the trail. Here they moiled for gold. You have to wonder if they found any.

It's a long pull up to Enni Camp. It might not seem as long if you camped at Mill Creek and broke the trip into two days to reach the lake. Trailhead to Papoose takes seven hours of steady walking.

Above Enni Camp you pretty much follow the outlet to the lake. Stay to the right of the huge gorge that develops below the lake. You may see rock "ducks" marking the trail. Knock them down so that those who follow will not be denied the wilderness experience you were cheated out of by the person who built them.

Spend some time at Papoose. After you leave, you'll wish to return soon. Get up on the divide and see that fabulous country west of Wedding Cake Peak. Take a dip in the lake and numb your body with the snowmelt from Mount Hilton. Stay up late and count stars. The world needs more star counters.

49

ROUND LAKE

Round Lake is like that throw rug in your hallway. It lays thrown over next to the hillside in the Deer Creek hallway.

It assumes its importance from the location. People making the loop of lakes around Siligo Peak can't help but check in on Round.

So Round sits there at the crossroads of Deer Creek. Anyone wanting to moniter the traffic in this area could not pick a better place to camp.

Evening comes early, morning late, in this deep canyon. The blue gash of sky between high forested walls; glaring gray granite on Seven-Up peak. The west is blocked out by 8162 foot Siligo Peak, the east by 8132 foot Seven-Up Peak. Summer days are short and hot, morning and evenings long and lingering. In winter, actual daytime is probably non-existent. Doubtful if there would be much traffic to monitor here in the winter.

Bill Horstman and I once camped near Round Lake. We found some old bed frames and springs that must have been left by some early mountain men. Seemed like a great idea to put our sleeping bags on the springs and sleep in the civilized comfort of a bed out here in the wilderness. Wrong! We were suspended in the cold night air which could pass not only over us, but under us too. We set jello out to cool under our makeshift spring beds. In the morn, both us and the jello were frozen and stiff from a night in the deep freezer.

Rush Creek Lakes. These three lakes are off by themselves, so are lightly fished. They are beautiful lakes, set deep between high granite walls. The two lower lakes are bordered by meadows, but the upper lake is completely rockbound and sometimes frozen over until August. A good trail leaves Kinney Camp, a four to five hour trip. The lakes can also be reached from the East Weaver Lake trail, by making your way to Monument Peak, then picking your way down the steep mountainside to the lakes. Both brook and rainbow trout in the upper lakes, brook trout in the lower lake.

LOWER RUSH CREEK LAKE

You can't find more beautiful slabs of granite entombing solitude than at Lower Rush Creek Lake. Be sure to come in from the Weaver Bally Road via Monument Peak. The trail up from Kinney Camp should be declared illegal. It must have been designed by a moron. Take it sometime and you'll see what I mean.

I sat in the fine meadow grass near here one endless summer day and wrote:
When warm summer days
that pass through your fingers
begin to cover
brittle pine needles
with unbelievable urgency,
sit down,
take your mind in your lap
use your memory like
a paring knife
to open your mind and place it
next to mine.
Carefully
remove the remnants of any
love that may cling in
anxious chunks to your childish thoughts
of me.
Place them in a bottle
seal it with sweat that
pools between your breasts sending
it to me by floating it on the sea.
It may be that it will

rise
with the mists, become clouds,
which rush themselves
to the mountains and spend themselves
panting for days
making love to the peaks.
The climax becomes the pure streams
that spill over
into the canyons
where I lie
on brittle pine needles
covered with the warm
summer days of that time
when we
both drank from the same stream
but
not really.

MIDDLE RUSH CREEK LAKE

> Middle Rush Creek Lake. Elevation 6,540 feet; 1 acre;
> 12 feet deep.

Middle Rush Creek Lake has a fine granite cliff on
one side. Get in the right place and bounce echoes.
One evening we lay on our sleeping bags at one end
of the lake and bounced .22 bullets off the lake to
hear them splat against the rock wall. That was years
ago, back when we carried guns into the alps to aid
us in our conquering efforts. It was us against the
wilderness in 1958. We were prepared to fight, if necessary, in order to return and report to Pres.
Jefferson what we had discovered in this part of the
Louisana Purchase.

Dixon Jones was our Sacajawea, our guide, in these
unknown hills. Seems like no matter where our Corps
of Discovery wandered, he had been there before.

Furthermore, he had Kodak slides at home to prove it. He had a mind and legs that none of us could match. Dixon never followed; he always showed us his heels. He had a story about the time he got mired down in the brush trying to use the trail on the map to Kinney Camp. Apparently it was an ugly struggle with the jungle-like brush in upper Rush Creek drainage. Dixon knew the idiocy of the Kinney Camp Trail.

> Upper Rush Creek Lake. Elevation 6,950 feet; 2 acres; 44 feet deep.

UPPER RUSH CREEK LAKE

Icebergs in August. That's Upper Rush Creek Lake. From the spring on Weaver Bally Road you can be on the lake in a little over an hour. The ice will be there even into late summer.

From East Weaver Lake head for the low gap to the north. Once in the gap, it is up over the right shoulder of Monument Peak. You'll pass within a few hundred feet of the summit so be sure and go on up and look around. Get the lay of the land. That is Upper Rush Creek Lake down there at your feet.

It may not be thawed out until July, but if it is thawed, you'll be able to catch fish.

Rush Creek Lakes are de facto wilderness. The area is rugged enough and obscure enough to protect itself so far. There seems to be nothing up there anyone wants. It may never be included in a wilderness area, but it's hard to imagine any exploitation of this fine granitescape.

The ridge that runs roughly south and east from the lake leads to two more secret and isolated pockets of solitude. These are nameless hideaways, seldom visited. Places you can spend a week and never see another human. Look for them below Peaks 7364 and 7060, north side, on your topographic map.

SAPPHIRE LAKE

There might be some places in this world too beautiful to describe. These places can only be experienced and tucked away in the mind for later dispensing to our senses.

Years ago, under the golden haze of a late afternoon in summer, Sapphire Lake was our Vallhala. We were viking gods and warriors riding our ships of granite boulders up the fjord. We stood on the prow of our rock boats and shouted praises to Odin.

The sky turned a deep turquoise blue, the lake was a piece of the sky, and as stars marked the limits of our visual universe, we built huge pyres of fire to feast on spaghetti and applesauce; swaggered drunk on flagons of Wyler's lemonade. The thoughts of future conquests and blond nordic encounters briefly troubled our sleep.

Sapphire Lake still gives the impression of being in a fjord. The vikings of 1958 are long gone, but the granite walls still leap upward, skyward, for thousands of feet. Even now, if you camp on the shores of Sapphire on a summer's eve, and don't build a fire, the quietness will stun. Listen closely enough, you'll hear faint echos, voices calling, "Odin."

The Know-It-All Guide labelled this lake as "Bottomless." Perhaps it is, in *many* ways.

Salmon Lake. Elevation 7,150 feet; 1.5 acres; 13 feet deep. Located at the head of the South Fork of the Salmon River. Reached by a beautiful and spectacular canyon ride that takes about four hours from Big Flat. The trail is clear and distinct to the divide between Willow Creek and the South Fork, then to the east there is a dim trail part way, but it is mostly a matter of picking your way to the lake. Stocked with brook trout.

SALMON LAKE

When you want to be alone, go to Salmon Lake. Weeks pass by, even in mid-summer, with no human voices breaking the silence. There is no trail. Only the highly motivated person will ever see this secret jewel embedded in the dark rock cliffs at the headwaters of the South Fork of the Salmon River.

You'll park at the Big Flat Campgraound even though a road goes three miles closer. For some un-justifiable, but equally mystifying, reason private interests have been allowed to maintain a road with a locked gate deep in this wilderness.

Walk south on the road, spit on the gate as you pass by. If enough of us do that, rust, which never sleeps, will eventually get rid of it.

Just past Gullick Creek, look for a trail to your left. Less than a mile later, watch for another fork at Kidd Creek, stay right this time.

After about four miles, you'll be wandering in the upper reaches of this fork of Salmon River. It is easy to lose the trail in this area, but it doesn't matter since the country is open and you can see where you have to go. Yup! Head for the low point on the sky-line dead ahead. The Trinity-Siskiyou county line.

The lake is over there at the base of Tri-Forest Peak (Shasta, Trinity, and Klamath National Forests at one time). Be sure to climb Tri-Forest while you're here.

You have to love this seldom seen view of Saw-tooth Ridge over to your right. Stunning granite spires. You can give each one your own name.

The meadow on the divide, the county line, is so wild, so beautiful, you'll never be able to describe it to anyone. So don't try.

SEVEN-UP LAKE

This is, along with Gibson, the other hide-and-go-seek lake. The lake was hidden several thousand years ago and your task is to find it. No trail.

The best way to start your search is to leave from Granite Lake and work your way at an upward angle along the red rock slides on the slopes of Seven-Up Peak. If you angle high enough, you'll find yourself above the lake and then can drop down to it. Lakes like this are much easier to spot from above, impossible from below.

When you leave Seven-Up lake, merely drop straight down to the trail along Granite Creek. If you decide to spend the night at the lake, rest assured you'll have the place to yourself.

How can the rocks here on Seven-Up Peak be so red, while across the valley and all the way up to Gibson Peak, are gray and white granite? Geologists call it a contact between two differing belts of rock types. California Division of Mines and Geology has several books and papers dealing with Trinity Alps geology. Those persons interested can look at it.

I find satisfaction enough in laying down on the sun warmed rocks and becoming a speck on a grain of sand in the universe, a microscopic flash in geologic eons. Looking out over Granite Creek Canyon, my eyes can soar like a hawk. Let others catalogue and classify the world.

Shimmy Lake. Elevation 6,400 feet; 1.5 acres; 10 feet deep. Because this lake is so open and shallow it gets rather warm during the summer. Reached by continuing on the trail past Eleanor Lake, or from Lily Pad Lake. Stocked with brook trout. Winter kill noted following severe winters.

SHIMMY LAKE

Shimmy is usually dead water with respect to fish, but it opens early in the spring and makes a great place to camp, swim and lounge about while exploring the Thumb Rock-Ycatapom country. As the summer wears on, the water warms.

Back in the old days when we still carried air mattresses, we would inflate them and navigate the lake as bare bottomed vikings. Fishing while prone on an air mattress can be a trick, too. We worked on the technique at Shimmy, but never really perfected it. Sit up and the mattress jackknifes in the middle. Then, should you hook a fish, it is difficult to release it while flat on your back.

Time was when Shimmy was a nice walk from Eleanor Lake with wide handsome views of Mount Shasta off to the east. Imagine! That hunk of mountain contains 80 cubic *miles* of material!

But Southern Pacific Land Company has spared you the trouble of walking to Shimmy Lake by building a road as close as they dared. They tried to improve the view by electing to cut down many of the larger trees that were "overripe" and cluttering up the place. The stumps remain for your enjoyment.

There used to be an interesting trail down from Deer Flat that would take you back to Gratton Flat to complete a nice loop. But the chaos of logging roads in the area has rendered it useless.

SMITH LAKE

What lake is the most beautiful in the alps? You may as well ask who is the most beautiful woman in the world. A task only to be undertaken by a fool. The Know-It-All Guide picked Smith Lake thus prejudicing the minds of a whole generation of alpsmen.

Alps lake beauty, like people, is in the eye of the beholder. It's only skin deep, and depends on how far away you are. All lakes are most beautiful, none is more so, none is less so. You could better spend your time contemplating the number of angels able to dance on the head of a pin.

Smith Lake is in the Stuart's Fork drainage, but don't be fooled. The only way to get there is via Canyon Creek (see comments under Morris Lake).

The place to camp is above the lake, on the inlet, so the big cliff overhanging the lake becomes your balcony. There you can sit or stroll morning and evening and keep tabs on the heavens and mountains around you.

There was a time when lack of a trail discouraged all but the most aggressive hikers to this lake. Now, the word is out and probably too many people visit Smith. Articles in *Sunset Magazine* have spoiled more than one beautiful place.

A few years ago a helicopter had to be used to rescue folks from the snowfields above the Canyon Creek approach. They were packing in a boat and supplies to cache until summer. A boat at Smith Lake is not necessary.

SNOWSLIDE LAKE

Here is the only lake in the Caribou Basin not named Caribou something. Apparently after big, little, upper, lower, and middle, they couldn't think of anymore prefixes for Caribou.

Snowslide is a pretty good choice of name. I'm sure. The Lake is right smack dab at the bottom of a steep slope that terminates at the summit of 8575 foot Caribou Mountain. You can bet plenty of snow slides down that slope.

It is at this lake you'll most likely lose the trail to Big Caribou. It's easy to do among all the little campsites and spur trails that litter the shoreline along the west side of Snowslide.

A lot of people wander too far to the west, go over and take a look at Lower Caribou, and then, realizing the trail has been lost, follow the stream rather than the trail up to Big Caribou.

Not that it matters a whole lot, but stay close to the shoreline of Snowslide as you pass by and you'll pick up the real trail at the south end of the lake.

I would advise camping here only if you enjoy life in the middle of a freeway. There are people back and forth through here day and night.

Little South Fork Lake. Elevation 5,950 feet; 9 acres; 21 feet deep. Located at the head of Little South Fork Creek, a tributary to the South Fork of the Salmon River. No trail. From the Salmon River side take the trail to the Caribou Basin; from where the trail leaves Ltitle South Fork Creek make your way up the creek to the lake. You'll encounter considerable brush. The terrain is very rough between the Caribou Basin and the lake. Stocked with rainbow trout.

LITTLE SOUTH FORK LAKE

There are several ways to reach this natural trout hatchery. All of them are tough. None can be recommended, but if you are dead set on catching huge fish, or want to step into a time machine and what the alps looked like 50, 75, even 175 years ago, then Little South Fork Lake should be on your list.

Gary Martin used to bust directly up Sawtooth Ridge from Emerald Lake, then drop down to L.S.F.L.. That's 3,000 feet up and 3,000 feet down in less than a mile. Devastating.

Some deranged souls find their way in from Caribou Basin. But what a price to pay. A long, killing contour around the headwaters of Middle Fork of Little South Fork followed by a 1500 foot up and down over a ridge to reach the lake.

I contoured in from Grizzly Lake once when snow levels were low. The elevation loss/gain was physically challenging. On the north side, this route always seems to have snow to some degree.

Dick Everest is probably right. There ain't no good way to get to L.S.F.L., but if you have to go, take the drive around to Cecilville and hike up the Little South Fork Trail until you cross the outlet stream. Follow the outlet stream, stay left at the waterfall, to the lake.

My Gawd! This is a tough lake.

SUGAR PINE LAKE

Sugar Pine is one of the secret places in the alps. And for good reason. The lake nestles at the head of a long, steep, soneway canyon. From the time you leave the trailhead on Coffee Creek until six miles later, when the lake is glimpsed through the trees, the trail climbs relentlessly.

Sure, there is trail that goes up over the ridge to the west, goes around the headwaters of Battle Creek, and drops into Union Creek, but no one ever uses it.

Sugar Pine is loaded with fish, has campsites that catch the early sun from the west, and normally nobody is camped there.

One of the pleasures of going to this lake is that you can concentrate on just going to the lake. No decisions to make about alternate routes or destinations. Once you leave the trailhead, you are committed to Sugar Pine Lake.

Notice the change of forest cover as you gain altitude, scattered oaks become scarce as the evergreens take over.

Notice the ridge lines on either side of the canyon. The one to the west has open green spaces while the east is more timbered with craggy rocks jagging the skyline.

Notice the meadows you pass through. Different sizes with different textures.

In late summer water along the trail is difficult to obtain. Try over to the left in the main stream.

The cirque holding the lake makes for interesting exploring as do the imposing cliffs to the west.

61

Summit Lake. Elevation 7,350 feet; 13 acres; 34 feet deep. Can be reached via the Long Canyon trail past Deer Lake, or by a dim trail from Diamond Lake. A scenic lake surrounded by broken boulders and sparse vegetation. Brook trout to 11 inches were caught in 1966. Rainbows also present.

SUMMIT LAKE

Summit Lake is aptly named. It appears to be a lake filling the top of a volcano when viewed from some angles. There is no inlet or outlet, leaving to your imagination how it maintains itself as a lake.

To get to Summit, you can travel one of the outstanding routes in all the alps: up Long Canyon, through Bee Tree Gap, and across Siligo Meadows.

From your car at the East Fork Trailhead, you are only five miles from the heart of the alps. Once you reach Bee Tree Gap and tire of the view eastward over towards Mt. Lassen, turn around, and behold, the alps are at hand!

Siligo Meadows at 7500 feet is lush and green. You might be put off by the cows that graze here late in summer, but the place is big enough to move elsewhere when you don't feel like a cowboy anymore.

When you tire of lounging about the treeless shore of Summit, the rock mass to the east (Peak 8059) is a rewarding stroll. Many people mistake this for Siligo Peak. Wrong! Siligo Peak is an interesting stroll to the north. Also worth your time to visit.

From either summit, while eating an orange, take a look around at this microcosm of the alps. Red rocks, gray/white granite, meadows, lakes, streams, snowbanks, stately snags and a sky close enough to touch.

Twin Lakes.

Lower Twin Lake. Elevation 5,000 feet; .25 acre; 2 feet deep.

Upper Twin Lake. Elevation 6,100 feet; .5 acre; 2 feet deep.

About ½ mile above the mouth of Granite Creek on the Swift Creek trail, Twin Lakes peak is sighted. Follow up the outlet stream for about one-half mile to the lakes, which have a small population of brook trout.

LOWER TWIN LAKE
UPPER TWIN LAKE

These lakes are really two brush-lined ponds. Nobody ever camps near them but I did once. Sometimes in the alps a person gets caught between places. Too late in the day to make it to your destination, but early enough to at least go someplace.

Twin Lakes are, at least, someplace. Leave the Swift Creek Trailhead and hike the easy mile to the Granite Lake Trail turnoff. Before the trail forks, you'll pass by that fantastic gorge where Swift Creek rips through sheer granite walls. Walls so vertical that even by leaning over the rim you can't see the creek below.

During low water of late summer, it is an adventure to enter this gorge from the lower end and explore up stream in the cool damp boulders. Fisherman can always get a few fish. Swimmers can always find a secluded place to dip in.

From the Granite Lake trail fork, stay right. In less than a mile the trail crosses a series of small seeping streams coming in from the right. This is the outlet of Twin Lakes. If the day is warm and you don't mind wet feet, the best way to find the lakes is to simply walk up the stream 'til you hit the lake. The The trees and brush are pretty thick, but with a little imagination, it is possible to avoid both wet feet and brush scratched faces.

You can catch a couple of Brook trout by using the hands and knees crawling approach with a fast retrieve.

63

UNION LAKE

The Union name you find scattered around this area comes from an early venture known as the Union Consolidated Mining Company.

As you hike up Union Creek it is easy to imagine the early road that ran through here with wagons and horses headed for the Dorleska Mine. Dorleska was the wife of R.D. Lawrence, discoverer of the mine in 1898. It soon went broke. The sixteen feet of winter snow no doubt helped speed the demise.

I once saw a photograph taken of a group of people at Union Lake in 1906. It is a contrast in timelessness. In the foreground the folks in turn-of-the-century dresses, huge floppy hats, wicker fishing creels, and a dog, sit, frozen in time. Behind them you can see the lake, the shoreline, the hillside exactly as it is today.

Perhaps this is the real message, the ultimate gift the alps can offer. Surely there is much to be learned from the simple idea that a true wilderness is timeless. It transcends the time and worlds of men.

A group of people in 1906 was able to have a wilderness experience in the framework of their lives just as the people of 1985 will. Nothing lasts forever, but the alps can last a lot longer than our short human lives. Thus it becomes a common thread of experience weaving through minds of men over hundreds of years. Envision if you can, the alpsman of 2281!

The hike to Union is easy, but philosophical.

WARD LAKE

During what geologists call the Wisconsin ice age, there were at least 30 valley glaciers in the alps. The longest glacier — thought to have been about 13.7 miles long — occupied the valley of Swift Creek.

The glacier left a really dandy route into Ward Lake. Oh sure, you could come in from Big Flat on a shorter steeper trail. If you are in a hurry, maybe you should.

But when you consider how long it took that last glacier to move down Swift Creek, any pace or route you choose will be meteoric by comparison.

Travel in Swift Creek Canyon is to be savored. It was an August 25 years ago when we trekked through the long shadows of a never-ending evening to a grassy knoll near the creek at Mumford Meadows. Sounds seemed to be muffled by the stillness of the air. And as night came on, we swore it was too warm for a sleeping bag. So we laid on top of our bags and peered deep into the space between the stars, talking of all the mysteries in the cosmos, and swapping lies to booster our young lives.

The next morning we found that the two or so miles to Ward Lake were laughingly easy for men as young and tough as we were. To prove it, on the way back to camp, we ran all the way nonstop.

Ward Lake or any part of the Swift Creek area makes for good running. Jog up from the trail head, spend the day, and jog back before dark.

EAST WEAVER LAKE

I read in an old copy of the local newspaper that in the 1880's a group of young people from town climbed up to East Weaver Lake and enjoyed an afternoon of ice skating. I was impressed. The walk from Weaverville to the lake would be a formidable undertaking to say the least.

A few winters ago I decided to take a look at the lake one cold day before snow had fallen — the kind of day when you fear your feet may become frozen to the ground.

Those early ice skaters knew what they were doing, going clear up there to skate. It may be that the best use of this lake is ice skating. The lake is on the north side of the ridge, insuring freezing conditions.

From late October until after Christmas, little snow falls during most years, yet it stays cold enough to keep a good sheet of ice on the lake.

The day I was there I beat a hole in the ice with the lug wrench I had carried from my truck just for that purpose. The ice was a good eight inches thick.

I built a little fire there by a log and, after the sun dropped and the blue shadows stole around the lake, that pinpoint of warmth combined with the frozen lake to make it seem as if it were 1880 once more.

East Weaver is a short hike from the Weaver Bally Lookout Road. The trail starts just above the spring.

TRAILHEADS

WHERE TO GET OFF

Stop at either the Weaverville or Big Bar Ranger Stations and pick up a Forest Service map. Shasta-Trinity National Forest. You could probably get one at the Supervisor's office, United States Forest Service, in Redding as well. This map will be much more current than your topographic maps making location of the trailheads much easier.

I will briefly describe only the *major* trailheads. If you will consult your Forest Service map, you'll see there are many opportunities for following a road to where it ends at the edge of a blank space on the map, park your car and plunge off into the wilderness.

Don't overlook the possibility of parking where a stream crosses the road and following that stream to its physical limit, or your physical limits.

BIG EAST FORK

(CANYON CREEK) This trailhead is impossible to find. But try turning right at the sign about 11 miles north of Junction City. Three miles up the dirt road, start looking for a road on your left. There may or may not be a sign. It might say "Maple Mine." It might say "East Fork Lakes." Most likely there will be no sign and you'll just get lost.

Parking is on the road shoulder. You can consult your topographic map and try to find the ridgeline north of the road. With a little luck you'll pick up the road/trail that leads to Buck's Ranch. From there the trail is obvious and steep.

BIG FLAT

Drive nineteen miles to the end of Coffee Creek Road. Park at Big Flat Campground. From here you can hit all Caribou Lakes, Josephine, Ward, Salmon, Horseshoe and Bullard's Basin. Preacher's Peak, Red Rock Mountain, Black Mountain, Tri-Forest Peak, Caribou Mountain and the north side of Sawtooth Ridge can all be reached from this trailhead.

BOULDER CREEK

About five miles up Coffee Creek Road, just past the Coffee Creek Ranch, look for a concrete bridge crossing the creek on your left. There may be a sign "Goldfield Campground." You may as well park just across the bridge as you can't depend on being able to drive much further.

The trail is obvious on the right hand side of the creek if going up Boulder Creek. *However*, there is a road/trail from here that eventually leads to Boulder Lake. I say eventually because it gets involved in a labyrinth of logging spurs and skid trails. You are advised to approach the Boulder Lake country from the Carr Road Trailhead.

The trail up Boulder Creek leaves the creek before the canyon ends. For a wilderness experience, stay with the creek, sans trail, up into Cub Wallow. Climb Peaks 8037 and 8081 and briefly be one with the wilderness.

CANYON CREEK

Thirteen miles north of Junction City. Drive to the end of the road past Ripstein Campground. Unfortunately there is plenty of parking and the place is usually full all summer long.

CARR ROAD

Drive north on Highway #3 about 38 miles from Weaverville. The road is not marked (1981), but it turns *sharply* left one fourth mile before you cross Coffee Creek. If you can't find it, ask at the Coffee Creek Ranger Station.

If you do find it, follow it about seven miles to where it ends at a logging landing. The trail may or may not be marked, but you can easily find it by sweeping south and west of the parking area.

On the way up the Carr Road you'll encounter several forks in the road. Always take the one that looks the most travelled if there is no directional sign.

CHINA CREEK

SOUTH FORK OF THE SALMON RIVER. Get headed out of Callahan towards Cecilville. After 28 miles of paved road, turn off left to East Fork Campground. About three miles later, watch for a road to the right. If you miss it, you'll come to Lor-O-Ranch and will have to backtrack. Once you get on the dirt road there are ample signs pointing the way to the trailhead. Parking is on the shoulder of the road. This is the trailhead to use for the Grizzly Lake country.

LONG CANYON

EAST FORK OF STUART'S FORK. North on Highway #3 at Covington's Mill, turn left just after crossing the creek. Watch for the sign. Trailhead is four miles up the road and is well marked. Not much parking space, but there never seems to be more than a few cars there at any one time.

From this trailhead the heart of the alps is readily accessible to those willing to toil for a few hours in Long Canyon.

GRANITE PEAK

About one half mile south of Mule Creek Guard Station on Highway #3 turn up the Granite Peak Road (across the highway from the road to Minersville and Bushytail Campgrounds). Follow the Granite Peak Road to the end. The trail leads directly up Granite Peak, into Red Mountain Meadows, Stonewall Pass and points beyond. It is steep all the way.

HOBO GULCH

Turn north immediately west of the Helena Bridge on Highway 299W. After several miles, watch closely for a sign and the road to the left that will wind up over Limestone Ridge and drop you into Hobo Gulch Campground. The trail is just uphill from the campground.

KINNEY CAMP

About ten miles north of Weaverville on Highway #3 you'll pass through a huge road cut and drop into a sharp hairpin turn to the right. In the middle of the hairpin a dirt road juts off to the left. It leads to a nice cold spring at Kinney Camp. The trailhead is a couple of miles past the camp. Watch for a sign. If you use this trailhead be warned: steep grades, no water until you get to the Lower Rush Creek Lake. It has a reputation among alpsmen as a real gutbuster.

LAKE ELEANOR

Thirty miles north of Weaverville on Highway #3, just over the Swift Creek Bridge, watch for sign and road to the left. Follow signs to the trailhead. About seven miles from the highway.

NORTH FORK SWIFT CREEK

Follow Lake Eleanor signs for about two miles but take the road to the right just over Gratton Creek. Follow signs. Trailhead is alongside the road past Lick Creek. Trail leads to Poison Canyon, Lilypad Lake, north face of Ycatapom Peak, and points beyond.

STONY RIDGE

This leads to a fine route into the alps via Stonewall Pass, past Red Mountain Meadows. However, the logging on Stony Creek and Granite Peak has been intensive. I think the place should be set aside as Logging National Park. The whole area is so ripped up that your best bet is to stop at the Weaverville Ranger Station and ask for current directions for finding this trailhead.

STUART'S FORK

This huge trailhead is at Bridge Camp Campground. A locked gate keeps you from driving another mile to Cherry Flat where the trail really begins.

At one time a road went all the way to Emerald Lake when the LaGrange Ditch was going full blast. The trail still follows portions of this old mining road.

Turn left just north of Stuart's Fork Bridge on Highway #3 fourteen miles from Weaverville. Follow the road right through the middle of Trinity Alps Resort. Don't be intimidated by the tourists at the resort; the road is a public thoroughfare. Continue past the horse stable two more miles to Bridge Camp.

SUGAR PINE

Drive up Coffee Creek beyond Coffee Creek Ranch watching for a sign on your left. Trail head starts just over the bridge on Coffee Creek. The trail leads to Sugar Pine Lake or over the ridge into seldom visited Battle Creek.

SWIFT CREEK

This is a big one! Swift Creek International Trailhead. A favorite with the horse crowd. Turn left just past the Swift Creek Bridge 30 miles north of Weaverville on Highway #3. Follow signs six miles to trailhead. The wilderness boundary is a mere 200 yards up the trail from the parking lot.

TODD CABIN

See directions to Hobo Gulch. On the way to Hobo Gulch watch for a sign on the right. The road drops down to the East Fork of North Fork, crosses it on a rather primitive bridge and peters out amongst mining claims in the area.

There are no lakes in this drainage, no trails and no people. It may not be proper to call it a trailhead when there isn't much of a trail.

Head up the East Fork of North Fork and you'll be writing your own script. It is untouched, unexplored country all the way to the Canyon Creek divide up on Mt. Hilton.

UNION CREEK

Watch for signs up Coffee Creek. There is parking for a couple of cars. Trail is to the south of the road. Actually the trail is a road for quite a ways. Back when the Dorleska Mine was a going thing there was a road all the way to Union Creek. A few years ago there was a forest fire near Union Lake and the P.F. Willies were able to punch their fourwheel drive vehicles almost to the lake.

WEAVER BALLY

Find Road north of Weaverville on the way to the high school. Follow road for about ten miles until you are out on the face of Weaver Bally. Watch for a small spring on your right. The trailhead is just beyond the spring. Parking is on the road shoulder. If you can't find it, proceed on to the lookout and inquire. There is always a foxy lady on duty during the summer. Trail leads to East Weaver Lake, Monument Peak, Rush Creek and Big East Fork.

EPILOGUE

EPILOGUE

So here it is, the culmination of a love affair I've had with the alps. It started out with innocent flirtations 25 years ago and ended up an all consuming mistress that demanded all the time and energy I could muster over the years. The passion was to visit every lake, climb every mountain. Now it's done. The book has been written.

The things we love become part of us. Perhaps it is not in the best interest of a wilderness area to publicize the place. Perhaps a wilderness area is doomed from the day it is defined as wilderness. By setting it aside, naming it, administering it, we bring a heretofore unknown wilderness to the attention of an uncaring public.

Is it not part of our western consciousness to tame wilderness. We came, we sawed, we conquered is the rally cry of the timber product companies. Should we pity the generations that will have no wilderness to tame?

But if wilderness becomes a condition of the mind and not a geographical area; a feeling we have for our world, our universe, then there will always be wilderness.

Millions of people have taken John Muir's advice; gone to the mountains and got "their good tidings." And yet the experience is not diminished. Each day of our lives is a first ascent.

Many beautiful and wonderful things have been destroyed in this world because of ignorance. Hopefully, this book might chip away a little at that ignorance.

I have starved, frozen and fried in these mountains; climbed the major peaks, drunk from every lake. One night two of us struggled by flashlight five miles to the car in a blizzard after abandoning our gear in the snow. One August I ran only in shorts and shoes from Big Flat to Trinity Alps Resort; clear across the alps practically naked in an afternoon. How many angles have I seen of Sawtooth Peak? Does love die when there are no more surprises? I'm compelled to return again and again. A yo-yo. I'm a cross between an alpsman and a Duncan Imperial.

I'm not alone. Many people know this place. I'm not surprised. Won't I ever get tired of this, weekend after weekend after weekend, summer after summer? Nope.

APPENDICES

STUFF TO READ

Cox, I., 1858, *The Annals of Trinity County*, 350 copies reprinted by John Henry Nash of University of Oregon, Eugene, Oregon, 1940, 265 p.

Diller, J.S., 1902, *Topographic Development of the Klamath Mountains*, U.S. Geologic Survey Bulletin #196, 69 p.

Eastwood, Alice, 1902, *From Redding to the Snowclad Peaks of Trinity County*, Sierra Club Bulletin 4:39-58.

Ferlatte, W.J., *A Flora of the Trinity Alps of Northern California*, 1974, University of California Press, 260 p.

Lipman, P.W., 1962, *Geology of the Southwestern Trinity Alps, Northern California*, Stanford University Ph.D. thesis, University Microfilms, Inc., Ann Arbor, Michigan, 210 p.

Sharp, R.P., 1960, *Pleistocene Glaciation in the Trinity Alps of Northern California*, American Journal of Science, V. 258, #5, p. 305-340.

Williamson, F.A., 1933, *The Unknown Alps of the Salmon River*, Sierra Club Bulletin 11.

Gass, C.L., 1976, *Regulation of Food Supply by Feeding Territoriality in the Rufous Hummingbird*, Canadian Journal of Zoology, V. 54, #12, p. 2046-2054.

The following items will suffice for May to October trips in the alps. Trips during other seasons will require another checklist. Consult a book on winter camping.

☐ pack/packframe
☐ day pack
☐ rain parka
☐ hat
☐ undershirt (2)
☐ long sleeve shirt (1)
☐ hiking shorts
☐ down parka
☐ socks (3 pr.)
☐ boots
☐ camp shoes/slippers/moccasins
☐ long pants (1 pr.)
☐ bandana
☐ sunglasses
☐ undershorts (2 pr.)
☐ shelter — tents are used in the alps only
   by green pilgrims and newlyweds
☐ bivouac cover/10'x10' plastic cover
☐ sleeping bag
☐ foam pad
☐ ground cloth
☐ pocketknife
☐ fork/spoon
☐ stove
☐ stove gas
☐ 1 quart bottle (plastic/aluminum)
☐ pot tongs
☐ emerycloth-backed sponge
☐ salt/pepper shaker
☐ matches (take a bunch)
☐ paper towels

- ☐ sierra cup
- ☐ frying pan
- ☐ plastic water container
- ☐ cooking pot(s)
- ☐ maps
- ☐ towel
- ☐ 50' cord
- ☐ snakebite/firstaid kit
- ☐ insect repellent
- ☐ stuff sack
- ☐ notebook/pencil
- ☐ small flashlight/batteries
- ☐ personal toilet articles
- ☐ camera/film (maybe?)
- ☐ fishing gear (maybe?)
- ☐ paperback book (maybe?)
- ☐ binoculars (maybe?)
- ☐ food
- ☐ Know-It-All Guide to the Trinity Alps

FUEL

Almost all your food for the alps can be purchased in super markets. Mountaineering stores will sell you over-priced, under-flavored concoctions that can only be marginally called food.

In the alps you eat what you want, when you want to. Forget that three-meals-a-day, no-snacks business. Fig newtons and tea with melted butter in it makes a dandy breakfast. Lunch starts just after breakfast and continues into supper. Supper blends right into bedtime. All meals are served one course at a time if you want them hot.

An alpsman travels on his stomach.

Look around the supermarket for these items and then compose your own menu. You'll need to repackage most of them.

prepared casseroles	honey/jam/peanut butter
applesauce	jello
bacon bar	milk/powdered
freeze dried meat	cooking oil
hard/dark bread	potatoes
crackers	puddings
margarine	spices
candy	salt/pepper
cereals	cookies (the staff of life
cheese	for the alpsman)
eggs/whole or powdered	cocoa/coffee/tea
nuts	drinks/powdered

RUNNING WILD

Nothing is closer to the wilderness ethic than running in the alps—running in any wilderness. No fires. Short stay as a visitor. Leaving only a few tracks, and darn fewer of them than a backpacker.

Discovering alps-running is like going from horse and buggy to jet plane. What used to be trips that took hours now only take minutes. What used to take days now only takes a few hours. There is no place in the alps that can't be reached and returned from in a single day if you run.

Only recently have I been keeping a log of running activities in the alps. Five miles/hour is good pace where the elevation gains approach 1000 feet per mile. Here are some samples of running times from trailhead:

Lower Canyon Creek Lake—70 minutes

Sugar Pine Lake—80 minutes

Granite Lake—60 minutes

Ward/Horseshoe Lake—two hours

Stonewall Pass—60 minutes

Thursday, August 2, 1979—Union Lake and Foster Lake (Bear). Union Creek is very gentle country—easy running. Before starting up last mile to Foster (Bear) Lake, take a good drink of water—no more water til lake.

August 17, 1979 — Long Canyon to Deer Creek and out Stuart's Fork to the boat ramp on Highway #3. Twenty-five miles in eight hours, of which seven were spent running/moving. What a day!

Saturday, July 14, 1979 — Canyon Creek Boulder Lake and Forbidden Lake (first time).
    aspen trees
    rare weeping spruce trees
    two hours from car to Forbidden Lake

Tuesday, July 31, 1979 — Alpine Lake
    surface water 70 degrees F.
    dirty campsites
    rare weeping spruce trees
    two hours five minutes from the car
    too steep to run last three miles before lake

Friday, June 20, 1980 (Julian Day 2,444,411) . . . my legs are pretty sore from running up to Granite Lake today. The azaleas were in full bloom along Swift and Granite Creek. I had the lake all to myself for awhile and then I worked my way up the red rocks of Seven-Up Peak to Seven-Up Lake. That makes lake #50 for me; only eight more to go and I'll have been to every lake in the alps. It was a fantastic day of sun, meadows, shaded trails and warm rocks. I wish I could do the same thing tomorrow . . .

Saturday, June 30, 1979 . . . got to Echo Lake by running up through Red Mountain Meadows, over Stonewall Pass and past Van Matre Meadows. After my visit to Echo Lake I ran/walked over Little Stonewall Pass to Siligo Meadows and a quick visit to Summit Lake. I looked down into Deer and Diamond Lakes.

With my present running abilities I'm able to cover ground that once took days. The day passed very rapidly as it seemed I was constantly moving. My faith in wilderness is restored. I spent the entire day, visited four lakes, covered about 18 miles of trail and still I didn't see a single soul! Saturday — first weekend in July — and not a person did I see!

Saturday, August 4, 1979 — the hardest trip I've ever tried to make in the alps was today — Mirror Lake via Canyon Creek. It is good running to the lower lake, then it is a scramble up to Ell Lake, a bush-whacking job to the saddle, and then loose, broken boulders down and over to Mirror. That is bad enough, but then you have to return over the same terrain. Mirror Lake will not be visited by many runners. I got the impression that it is not often visited by anyone. I sure love to run in Canyon Creek. Took several dips in the creek on the way back.

Friday, August 10, 1979 — you never see any fat people in the alps.

Wednesday, July 23, 1980 (Julian Day 2,444,444) . . . at 10:20 a.m., Julie and Wayne, Jr. let me off at the locked gate below Carter's resort at the head of S. Fork Salmon River and I was off. In less than two hours I was at the Divide between Salmon and Willow Creek. Took a side trip to look at Salmon Lake, #51 on my life list, and then I was down into Willow Creek. But that divide between S. Fork Salmon and Willow Creek will have to go down as one of the most beautiful places in the alps. It is a long, wide meadow that slopes up and meets the jags of Sawtooth Ridge. It is just wild, lonely and beautiful. From this high meadow it was a long downhill run to where I left the truck at the Stuart's Fork Boat Ramp. I stopped at

Morris Meadows for a dip in the creek and then as the afternoon wore on and I wore down, I stopped and dipped in the creek several times. It was cool blue color and 58 degrees F. My legs were getting pretty numb by the time I got to the truck, but the 3 cans of Diet Pepsi I inhaled helped relieve the discomfort.

Friday, August 17, 1979 — sometimes even this old woodsman bites off too big of a chunk. Julie dropped me off at the Long Canyon Trailhead and I took off running. Seven hours later, with very sore legs, I stopped running. It was up Long Canyon to Bee Tree Gap, Deer Lake, Summit Lake, Diamond Lake, Luella Lake, Round Lake, and then down Deer Creek to Morris Meadows, and eventually on out to Stuart's Fork Boat Ramp. The hardest part, I think, was going by the dining hall at Trinity Alps Resort after six and one half hours of running. It smelled good!

This very same trip I took 21 years ago, in 1958, only Bill Horstman and I spent three *days* doing it with packs on our backs. Now, 21 years older, I did the same thing, alone, in eight hours total time (seven hours and fifty minutes).

My legs feel like limp noodles after a marathon. I probably covered 25 miles today.

Tuesday, August 21, 1979 — ...I took a good run up Canyon Creek...It was cold, wet, in the alps, not very friendly. Usually when I'm in the mountains I'd like to pull the trail in behind me and stay there forever. But on a day like today I'm glad that my visit is going to be temporary. A wilderness can be wicked and forbidding on a stormy day.

I came upon places that hold warm day memories

and find it hard to picture that it was ever real when the rain is beating down cold on the rocks while clouds rumble and gurgle overhead.

Wednesday, August 22, 1979 — nighttime, Grizzly Lake. I've sat and stared into a lot of campfires, but none as soft and quiet as this one is. My own thoughts are as still as the glowing embers, pulsating with the heat, burning and consuming themselves as the darkness closes in around us, me and my fire at Grizzly Lake.

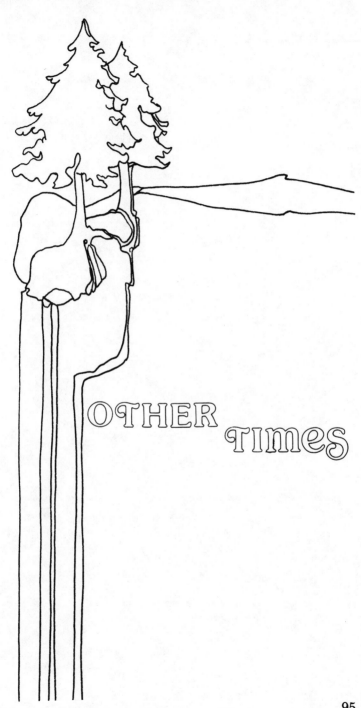

OTHER TIMES

FROM REDDING TO THE SNOW-CLAD PEAKS OF TRINITY COUNTY;*

ALSO,

LIST OF TREES AND SHRUBS SEEN EN ROUTE.†

By Alice Eastwood.

In August, 1899, Dr. C. Hart Merriam, Chief of the United States Biological Survey, and his assistant, Mr. Vernon Bailey, made a scientific exploration of these little-known mountains which form part of the northern boundary of Trinity County and from which the chief branches of Trinity River take their rise. These scientists reported unusual physical features, wildness and grandeur of scenery undreamed of, and, besides, brought back a small but very interesting collection of plants from the summits of the ridges; so that it seemed as if life would lose its zest if these mountains could not be reached, their rugged peaks climbed, their botanical treasures collected, and their dangers and difficulties overcome. Our party consisted of Mr. S. L. Berry, Mr. Carlos T. Hittell, Dr. Kaspar Pischel, and the author.

Neither mules nor burros were to be had in Redding and we were compelled to take horses. The horses that we obtained at the stable of Vannah & Saunders were so poor as to be a disgrace even to the pack-horse tribe. They were on their last legs and gave us great trouble and delay, almost causing the complete failure of the trip.

We left Redding about ten o'clock the morning of July 2d, leading our extremely quiet beasts, planning where we would be by night, and indulging in dreams of at least twenty miles a day.

The first day out we passed through a rolling country where occasional small streams crossed the road, some of them containing a little water, but most of them dry. The road was very dusty, as is usual at this time of the year; but the oldest inhabitant never remembered to have seen the dust so bad as this year. This was caused by the increased freighting which the development of the Sweepstake Mine is inducing. It was the country of the digger pine (*Pinus Sabiniana*), which found no breeze in which to wave its gray-green plumes. The pale gray manzanita (*Arctostaphylos viscida*) everywhere prevailed, forming great bushes almost treelike. Along the stream-banks and in the beds of dry streams the button-willow (*Cephalanthus occidentalis*) was in full bloom and refreshed the eye with its bright green foliage and its globular heads of whitish flowers, while its fragrance perfumed the air as we passed some distance away. Now and then a bush of redbud (*Cercis occidentalis*) was seen, with its clean, round, green leaves and its purple pods. *Quercus Wislizeni* is the live-oak of the region. It forms round, compact trees with holly-like leaves. There were besides, the blue oak (*Q. Douglasii*) and the black oak (*Q. Californica*). *Ceanothus integerrimus* and *C. cuneatus* were the most common species of Californian lilac, the former having loosely-flowered panicles of white or pale blue flowers, and bright green alternate leaves, the latter with rigid opposite branches, small gray-green wedge-shaped leaves, and small compact clusters of white flowers all over the stems when in bloom in the spring. Poison-oak climbed over the bushes or grew in clumps and was already beginning to turn red. *Rhamnus Californica* (the coffee-berry) was common and gave promise of much fruit. Everywhere the wild grape hung in graceful festoons over the trees or clothed fences. Occasionally *Clematis ligusticifolia* climbed over the bushes, and was seen either in full bloom with its panicles of starlike, white flowers, or with the globular heads of seeds beginning to be plumose. Poplars and alders grew along the streams.

As we approached Shasta, an old mining town, *Pinus attenuata* and *P. ponderosa* began to appear, and in some places the valley oak (*Quercus lobata*) was noted, though not so common nor so fine as in localities where the soil is richer and more moist. Between Shasta and Whiskytown *Cupressus Macnabiana* was found, perhaps the locality where this cypress was first discovered. As we climbed the hill separating these two places, once the scenes of great activity, wild revelry, and wasted lives, now dead and deserted, new trees and shrubs were seen, the big-leaved maple of the Pacific Coast (*Acer macrophyllum*), the buckeye (*Æsculus Californica*), the wild cherry (*Cerasus demissa*), the wild plum (*Prunus subcordata*), the sweet shrub (*Calycanthus occidentalis*), *Styrax Californica*, the mock orange (*Philadelphus Gordonianus*), several species of dogwood, all so covered with dust as to be scarcely recognizable. From the top of this hill a fine view of the whole country can be seen, the Sacramento Valley lying to the east, the mountains to which we were traveling to the northwest, while to the northeast Mt. Shasta loomed up grand and solitary, twice as high as any other mountain.

It was about six in the evening when we reached Whiskytown. As we could buy food for the horses at the stable and there was a fine spring near the bridge and a level place adjacent, we decided to make this our first night's camp.

The next day was hot and the road very dusty. We passed several freighting-wagons, canvas-covered and drawn by from four to ten animals. The most beautiful place on the road is the well-known Tower House, a haven of rest, coolness, and shade. Great trees spread their branches over the road, which is kept free from dust by the frequent use of the hose. Long ago *Melia Azedarach* was planted through this country as a shade-tree, and has become thoroughly naturalized. Young trees were seen everywhere as we traveled along the road.

We had heard of a trail not far from here that led to Lewiston, and we longed to reach it, so as to be out of the horrible dust. It was on this trail, by the side of a stream of good water, that we made our noon camp. It was a beautiful place, full of trees, beneath which the white flowers of the *Philadelphus* gleamed in their purity; the tropical-looking *Aralia* grew luxuriantly in wet places, but was not yet in bloom; the buckeye and redbud, the maples and oaks abounded through the little valleys and on the adjacent hills. Tiger-lilies bordered the streams in places, and the bright scarlet California pink peeped from under the shrubs. The trail led to the summit of a high hill from which Mt. Shasta was again visible.

It was here that "Tom" gave out and seemed to be scarcely able to walk; so we decided to camp where we first found water and see whether it would be possible to obtain another horse at Lewiston, which was distant about five miles.

After much trouble, many discouragements, and a delay of a day and a half, a young mare was obtained from Mr. William Hampton, of Lewiston, and we left the old horse in a pasture until our return. This mare proved to be a valuable animal, sure-footed, accustomed to keeping free from the rope when tied, and determined to neglect no opportunity to graze either on the trail or in the pasture.

Dr. Pischel, whom we expected to meet at Weaverville, was intercepted at Lewiston, and came to our camp in the cañon instead of going on.

This cañon was one of the loveliest places and the most interesting to a botanist of any that we passed on the way to Cañon Creek. Here *Philadelphus* was glorious, the vine-maple (*Acer circinatum*) was common; one tree of the chestnut-oak (*Quercus densiflora*) was noted, the only one seen on the trip; the rare *Ribes Lobbii* was seen for the first time; *Cornus sessilis* was in fruit, and the most beautiful of all the honeysuckles of California (*Lonicera ciliosa*) held out its flame-colored flowers over the bushes like a torch to illumine the darkness of the cañon in the shade of evening, when it was first seen, a surprise and a never-to-be-forgotten delight. The California yew (*Taxus brevifolia*), the incense cedar (*Libocedrus decurrens*), the fir (*Abies concolor*), the yellow pine (*Pinus ponderosa*), the sugar pine (*P. Lambertiana*), were all there, while the Douglas spruce (*Pseudotsuga mucronata*) reached a fine development and fruited most abundantly. Madroños and alders, maples and oaks prevailed amid these other trees.

It was on the afternoon of July 5th that we reached Lewiston, a small farming town on the Trinity River. From there we went by trail to the summit of a hill separating Lewiston from Weaverville, and camped at a beautiful upland meadow known as Packer's Camp. It was about sunset when we arrived, and Mt. Shasta was in the glow of the setting sun. Wherever this mountain appeared, it rose like a giant over the other mountains which were to be seen on every side. Here again we met beautiful sugar pines. The generally prevalent black oak was replaced by *Quercus Garryana*. This upland meadow was like a park, the rolling surface, " tanned by summer's breath," formed a fine background for the beautiful oaks and the picturesque pines. From the western summit we saw distinctly for the first time the mountains for which we were aiming; but it was not until we had learned their outlines by intimate acquaintance that we knew them to be the same.

At last, about 10 on the morning of July 6th, we reached Weaverville, a day and a half after the expected time. This is the county seat of Trinity County and one of the few towns of '49 which is still flourishing. Before noon we climbed the hill which separates the town from the La Grange Mine. It was hot and dusty beyond any place that we had passed, for we were approaching the goal of all the freighting-wagons. When we at last reached water we were too tired, hot, and thirsty to eat, and made but few preparations for lunch. In the afternoon we passed the great La Grange Mine, where the hydraulic giants were washing away the mountains and filling the river-bed below with an artificial moraine of rocks and débris. It is desolation and ruination of the natural features of the country, and the result on the landscape is typical of the effect on humanity of the greed for gold.

Late in the evening we reached Anderson's ranch, the first place near Junction City where we could obtain pasture for our horses, wood, water, and a place to camp. About eight the next morning we passed Junction City and another big placer mine, owned by a French company. We were now on Cañon Creek, the stream which we were to explore to its source. From the first it was most interesting and beautiful. In one place it had worn a labyrinthine course through the solid rock, in other places it was bounded by clifflike walls, while the banks opposite were bordered with fresh green trees and shrubs, untainted by the dust of the road. Here I saw the only bush of azalea that was noted on the entire trip. Blackberries and black raspberries were quite common, and were ripening. We often stopped to eat the fruit. It was along this road that we came across several colonies of Chinese engaged in placer mining with all the modern methods—hydraulic giants, pipes, and flumes. Now and again we walked through old placer washouts where the trees had begun to reassert their sway. Occasionally we passed a lonely cabin in which some old miner lived. These men seemed like the driftwood of humanity left behind on the great tide that swept over the country in the days of '49. They were chatty and liked to talk of olden times. There seemed to be traces of deserted ranches everywhere, represented by fruit-trees uncared for, but usually having a small crop of apples or peaches.

At last, about 6 in the evening, we reached the small town of Dedrick. This was the terminus of civilization, and the next day would find us in the unknown country which we had come so far to see.

We were told of a place up the cañon where we could get pasture for our horses, but were misdirected and went about a mile up the steep grade to the Chloride Mine before finding our mistake. It was late when we reached the camp, tired and hungry, and with the horses ready for a better feed than the scanty pasture promised.

Very little seemed to be known of the trail or the cañon by the people whom we asked. They told us that we would have difficulty in fording the creek, that the fords were many and, at this time of the year, dangerous, and that the trail would be hard to find, on account of being overgrown with brush and obstructed by fallen trees.

The next morning, however, we started early with brave hearts but with many misgivings. One or more generally went ahead to explore while the others stayed behind with the animals, and we all took turns at leading the beasts. There were altogether seven fords from Dedrick to the upper lake. Every one was a horror to me; but the men roped the animals over without any accidents, and at all except one we found logs on which to cross. One log was especially shaky and dangerous. It was high above the water, which formed a pool twenty feet deep below.

All through this beautiful cañon, rare and lovely flowers grew. Five species of the dainty *Pyrola*, two species of *Campanula*, the rare ghost-orchid, *Cephalanthera*, *Chima-*

phila, Vancouveria, all flourished in the shade of the forest. *Clintonia uniflora* carpeted the ground in shady places where the hot sun could not wilt its pure white, starlike flowers. The rare *Lewisia cotyledon* was seen for the first time near one of the fords, strikingly beautiful, bearing panicles of bright pink flowers.

The first falls are the best known, as few people go any higher. This fall we christened "Hound's-Head Fall" from a rock shaped like a hound's head, which jutted out on one side as if looking into the cataract. From there on, the creek was a succession of most lovely cataracts, any of them more beautiful than the falls near the forks of Bubbs' Creek in the King's River country.

We were two days in reaching Twin Lakes, a distance of nine miles. We had to cut trails through the brush; for we completely lost the trail in one place, having been led astray by some predecessor. It was a wild country that we were approaching—granite peaks clothed with snow, but with trees even to their summits, lakes of great beauty, and creeks and waterfalls everywhere. Here we saw for the first time the weeping spruce (see photograph), one of the rarest trees in California, though more common in Oregon. It is a singular-looking tree, and would attract attention anywhere. The tree is pyramidal in general outline, but rarely symmetrical: it is branched from the base with horizontal branches. From these branches the branchlets hang like long thick fringe from one to several feet in length. The tree has the appearance of being draped or veiled with these slender branchlets. The cones hang from the upper branches, and the old ones persist after having discharged their seeds.

From Redding to Twin Lakes we had passed three zones of trees, the first represented by the digger pine (*Pinus Sabiniana*), the second by the sugar pine (*Pinus Lambertiana*), and the third by the mountain pine (*Pinus monticola*). The gray-green manzanita (*Arctostaphylos vis-cida*), which had prevailed where the digger pine grew, overlapped into the zone of the sugar pine. In this zone, *Arctostaphylos patula*, the manzanita with smooth, bright green foliage and large berries, was the common species. This also overlapped into the zone of the mountain pine, but was uncommon, being replaced by the low manzanita which clings to the rocks or spreads like a mat over the ground, known as *Arctostaphylos Nevadensis*. In the upper regions this manzanita was in flower, gemmed with the clusters of pearl-like, pure white flowers. The yellow pine reached the zone of the mountain pine, but Douglas spruce had been left some distance behind down the cañon. A few storm-beaten and most picturesque trees of *Libocedrus decurrens* were seen all along the trail from Dedrick to the lakes. Fine specimens of hemlock-spruce (*Tsuga Merten-siana*) grew on the banks of the lakes and high up on the mountains to the summits of the ridges. In the neigbor-hood of the lakes the red fir (*Abies magnifica Shastensis*) (see photograph) was common.

Beautiful shrubs grew all around. *Bryanthus empetri-formis* formed mats of mountain heather laden with deep rose-colored bells. *Leucothœ* and *Ledum* flourished in the swamps together with the mountain ash, the wild cherry, the meadow-sweet, the small-flowered bush-honeysuckle (*Lonicera conjugialis*), and all were in full bloom. The most abundant shrub seemed to be *Ceanothus velutinus*. This formed the most disagreeable brush to penetrate where there were no trails; for it grew so tall and so rank and with such unyielding stems. The fragrance of its foliage added to that of its flowers made it attractive in spite of being so great an obstacle to our progress. The mountain maple (*Acer glabrum*) grew along the lakes, and what seems to be a new species of fringe-bush, or *Garrya*, was common. The low-spreading oak (*Quercus vaccinifolia*) clothed the rocks of the talus almost to the summit of the ridges; more often it helped instead of hindering our progress. A peculiar shrubby yew was also abundant in places, forming dense thickets. From the time that we left the last madroño, near the foot of Hound's-Head Fall, we had gone from a flora very similar to that of the coast under the redwoods and had reached one subalpine in character, within a distance of less than nine miles.

We passed great slopes of granite polished by glacial action to almost the degree that granite is polished for monuments or buildings. Glacial scratchings were everywhere and big rounded bowlders frequent. Piles of talus almost covered by brush seemed to prevail on the eastern side of the cañon; but in the main amphitheater, the smooth granite covered great areas. Higher up the granite became sharper in the outline of the bowlders and cliffs. There was an awfulness about the summits that was forbidding. The ridge was a succession of pinnacles and cliffs—a regular Sierra. Not one of the peaks was easy climbing at the top.

Our camp lay about a quarter of a mile below the lowest lake, a short distance from the trail and not far from a small stream of ice-cold water which came from the snow-banks of the mountain on the east. It was in the open, on the rocks. We camped here because in the meadow below there was good feed for the horses. We were dry and much warmer at night on these rocks and almost free from the mosquitoes and other insects which were a pest in the wet meadow below. To be sure, we had no shade, but we did not expect to be in the camp by day, and at night it made no difference. Every evening we watched the rays of the sun leave one peak after another, and that on which they rested longest we named Sunset Peak. From behind the next peak to the south the planet Jupiter rose after sunset and made a beautiful picture in the evening sky; so we named this mountain Mt. Jupiter. The sky was wonderfully clear, and all the summer constellations shone out with great distinctness; the Milky Way and the Scorpion on one side, the Great Bear and Perseus on the other, while Vega and Corona were in the zenith above.

The birds were numerous and very musical. Never have I heard so many songs as greeted us every morning about the break of day. We saw linnets, thrushes, and water-ouzels. I heard one of the last chirping gayly as he danced in and out of a cataract where he was looking for insects. Small game seemed to be scarce. We saw a few grouse—scared up one mother bird on a nest of five eggs.

The first expedition was to attempt the ascent of Thompson's Peak (see photograph), the highest mountain of the group. The ridge was ascended on the western side of the upper lake to the summit. It was very steep and rough; in some places great tracts of snow had to be crossed, and when the summit of the ridge was reached, the succession of cliffs, pinnacles, and knife-edges that intervened between the point to which we had ascended and the peak which seemed the highest showed that it was too late in the day to begin to make an attempt to reach it, even if it were at all possible from that side.

The peak which we climbed to the summit was that which we had named Sunset Peak (see photograph). We started from our camp at its foot and made the ascent along the course of the stream and the snow-banks. Every step was an upward one, but not dangerous, though to look back upon the course by which we had come made one dizzy with its precipitous slope. We kept out of the snow as much as possible, climbing over the talus whenever we could. Beautiful flowers bloomed where the snow had melted a few days before. Beds of crimson *Bryanthus*, clumps of *Anemone occidentalis*, with large flowers as white as the snow which had so recently covered them, *Saxifraga*, *Arnica*, *Caltha*, *Trifolium*, *Aster*, *Erigeron*, *Potentilla*, *Aquilegia*

Pentstemon, *Mimulus*, *Tofieldia*, and *Hastingsia*. On the summit of the ridge we found *Cassiope* in full bloom, a yellow-flowered *Draba*, a beautiful *Pentstemon*, and even up here the hardy hemlock-spruce had climbed, one little tree being found laden with purple cones.

From the summit of the ridge to the summit of the peak the ascent was made over great blocks of granite, but none so high as to be climbed with any difficulty. Mr. Hittell was ahead, and had climbed a cliff from which he could not descend. How he had managed to get up with his camera on his back was a mystery. Mr. Berry and I used a rope to make the ascent to the top of the rock on which Mr. Hittell sat, and from there to the summit it was easy work. The most beautiful view of Mt. Shasta was had on the way up this cliff. To see this mountain at its best it must not be seen from too near, for its immensity does not impress one on account of the absence of anything with which to compare it. It must not be seen from too far, as I saw it once from the top of Mt. St. Helena, for its outlines are too dim; but from the distance and elevation of these mountains, its great size and its grandeur as a mountain can never be forgotten.

From the top of this peak we had a chance to see the country near at hand and decide what parts to explore before we had to return. On all sides were amphitheaters at the foot of rugged granite peaks similar to that on which we stood. Great snow-covered slopes spread between these crests and lost themselves in green meadows and dashing torrents. We rolled some rocks down on to one of these snow-banks and started an avalanche. We could hear the swish of the snow a thousand feet below and looked down upon this torrent of snow as it sped swiftly along, with the snow on each side as unmoved as the rocky banks of a river. The peak which rose beside the one on which we stood seemed to be the higher, but we had no instruments by which we could tell and had no time to make the ascent; so we took a picture of it to show the general character of these rocky summits. Mr. Berry went down the way that we had come up, jumping from the cliff to a snow-bank below. Mr. Hittell and I returned by the other side, and soon found that it was not so easy as it promised. After about an hour of careful work and the almost constant use of the rope, we managed to reach a place where the descent was easy.

Our next expedition was to the foot of Thompson's Peak, or what we took to be that mountain. This is a cone-shaped peak, apparently difficult to climb, and would have taken two days from our camp. We did not have the time, and gave it up. There was no trail above the upper lake, and we had to make our way through the brush. We kept up, but found on the return that it would have been easier to have skirted the eastern edge of the lake as closely as possible. On the western side the rocky cliffs come down to the water, and it is not possible to go on that side without climbing half-way up the mountain. The water in the streams above the second lake was the purest that I have ever seen. It flowed over granite that was almost as white as snow, and every pebble could be counted at the bottom of pools and streams. Here the willows were beginning to bloom, the *Kalmia* still held its pink flowers, and *Dicentra uniflora* had not disappeared.

The day after, we devoted to the exploration of the western amphitheater which we had seen from Sunset Peak. We found this full of little lakes on two benches. The lower bench held a cluster of four or five, more or less in a chain; the upper a pair of twin lakes almost surrounded by snow-banks. We stood under one snow-bank more than ten feet high.

It was on the way up here that we saw a bear. Mr. Hittell was ahead sketching; I was in the rear. Mr. Berry called to me to come quickly. On the opposite side of the stream which came from the lower chain of 'lakes, walking along a bench of rock on the side of the cliff, was a big cinnamon bear, not fifty yards away. He looked at us undisturbed and we looked at him. We tried to call to Mr. Hittell, but he was too far ahead; the sound of the cataracts deadened our voices, and he did not understand our signs. Mr. Berry had only a 38-caliber Smith & Wesson, but he shot at the beast and really hit him, for the bear shook his head and his paws and trotted on. The sting of a small bullet at the distance was probably no more than the sting of an insect. Again Mr. Berry shot, and this time the bear became really scared, turned, and ran off as fast as he could in the direction whence he had come. Mr. Hittell's chagrin was great when he learned what a chance he had missed.

The next day, July 15th, we began the return trip. We had no difficulty in finding the trail or in getting over the fords, and in consequence were only a day in returning to Dedrick. From there on, the journey was without incident. Near Lewiston we gave up the mare with regret and again took Tom, apparently as stiff and lame as when we left him in the pasture two weeks before. We were two days and a half in reaching Redding, but rejoiced that we got him there alive.

The easiest and quickest way to reach these mountains is by stage to Dedrick. The journey takes two days from Redding. We were uncertain about getting pack-animals at Dedrick, therefore we packed from Redding and walked.

110

THE UNKNOWN ALPS OF THE SALMON RIVER

By Frank A. Williamson

❧

THE interior of northern California includes a portion of the Coast Range Mountains which is comparatively unknown, because of its present inaccessibility. A study of the Shasta quadrangle of the United States Geological Survey shows Mount Eddy, with an elevation of 9151 feet, at the head of the Trinity Mountains. Parallel to the Trinity Mountains, at a distance of about twenty miles to the west, are the Salmon Alps, and, connecting the two, a transverse ridge known as the Scott Mountains. The drainage between these mountain ridges forms the watershed of the Trinity River, with Coffee Creek, Swift Creek, and Stuarts Fork as main tributaries from the Salmon Alps on their eastern slope. The trend of the main ridges is north and south. The Salmon Alps on their western slope drain into the Salmon River, and their backbone forms part of the boundary between the Trinity and the Klamath national forests.

WE START FOR WEAVERVILLE, IN TRINITY COUNTY

The most convenient railroad station to reach this alpine country is Redding, Shasta County, on the Southern Pacific Railroad. From Redding a fifty-five mile automobile ride over mountain roads brings us to Weaverville, in Trinity County. Leaving Redding by automobile at five in the evening, we travel along the macadamized State Highway to its present termination at Tower House on the road to Weaverville. The latter point is the county-seat of Trinity County, headquarters of the Trinity National Forest, and starting-point of hunting, fishing, and mountaineering expeditions into the rugged interior.

To reach Weaverville three roads are available from Tower House to Lewiston on the Trinity River. One road leads by way of French Gulch and Deadwood to Lewiston, and is known as the Tom Green Grade. Another road branches off one mile beyond Tower House. One of these branches, known as the Toll Road, leads directly to Lewiston; the other branch reaches Lewiston by way of Lowden's Ranch. The latter road, also known as the Buckhorn Grade, has been chosen as the route of the State Highway to be extended in the near future from Tower House to Lowden's Ranch and on to Douglas City. Our choice is the Tom Green Grade, and we reach Weaverville by way of Lewiston and across Brown Mountain at eight in the evening, after three hours' travel from Redding.

A FRENCH DINNER IS SERVED

An unexpected treat in the way of a French dinner is served at the hotel, prepared by Louis Gaston, the chef, who through some freak of fate finds himself and his cuisine transplanted to Weaverville from the bay region.

The following morning, at Forest Service headquarters, we secure all available data and maps regarding the area to be entered, incidentally viewing some of the buildings and landmarks of early history, described so attractively in John Carr's book, "Pioneer Days in California."

In the meantime pack-animals previously arranged for are being loaded by the capable hands of John Quincy Adams, guide and packer, and his half-breed assistant, Joe. After the usual but unavailing protests of the animals the pack-train starts at last for Kenny Camp, twenty miles distant by automobile, twelve miles by pack-trail.

OLD BRUIN RIDES IN A TRUCK

Our party follow in machines, retracing our way up Brown Mountain toward Lewiston, then taking a branch road leading up Rush Creek toward Junkan's Ranch and Minersville. At the Rush Creek bridge a rather steep mountain grade branches off the main road and crosses the ridge to Kenny Camp, the starting-point of the pack-trail and the end of automobile travel. The road itself continues down into the cañon, and after crossing the Stuarts Fork of the Trinity River terminates at Goetze's Ranch (Adams' Ranch on old maps). Having been delayed by gasoline feed troubles, when we finally reach Kenny Camp we find the pack-train already encamped. We are told all about a bear, of which this country has an unusually large number, this particular bear creating a diversion by stampeding the pack-animals on the way over, thus adding to the pleasures of life for Mr. John Quincy Adams, guide and packer. Our mirth is great when we hear that old bruin was riding in an auto-truck and inside a cage, as part of a traveling circus bound for Minersville.

As it is too late to continue to Bridge Camp, we stay here till

112

morning. A clearing on a knoll a short distance up the trail is our choice for bedding-ground, as it offers a magnificent view of Castle Crags in the distance.

THE HIKE TO MORRIS MEADOWS

At daybreak we abandon our machines at Kenny Camp, not to hear or jump at the sound of an automobile horn for ten days. The pack-animals having been properly loaded, we start on our sixteen-mile hike to the head of the Stuarts Fork and Morris Meadows.

Crossing a low knoll to an abandoned mining-ditch serving as trail, we follow this ditch to within a mile of Bridge Camp, five miles up-stream. As we travel along the winding ditch, openings in the brush and timber growing on the cañon slope yield an occasional glimpse of Stuarts Fork with its turbulent cascades a thousand feet below us. Glancing down-stream we secure a vista of Goetze's Ranch with its green meadow and timbered mountain background.

Where the trail rounds a jutting spur after leaving the ditch, a bear hustles down hill and disappears in the manzanita and buck-brush, rolling over and over. Through the trees ahead of us we can see extensive fields of snow on glistening granite crags against a jagged skyline, holding forth the promise of cool days and cooler nights, after the semi-tropical summer temperatures of the Great Valley of California. At this point the trail drops zigzag down the cañon-side to the delight of those traveling by shank's mare, and the discomfiture of the mounted members of our party, who are forced to dismount and coax their animals on their hesitating way down-hill.

We ford the Stuarts Fork for Bridge Camp on the opposite bank, where we find the abandoned site of a construction camp, not in use since the days when the La Grange Mining Company battled against the forces of nature and the difficulties of high finance, and found the struggle too severe. An inverted steel syphon, now abandoned, crosses Stuarts Fork on a trussed bridge. Twisted and torn steel plates half an inch thick bear mute evidence of the destructive force of water when confined under pressure.

AN EIGHT-POINT BUCK SWIMS ACROSS THE STREAM

After a short breathing spell we continue along the banks of the stream, its murmuring cascades and mystic green pools sounding a persuasive refrain, calling to us to cast our trout-fly. A deer breaks from the buckbrush at our side and swims across the stream, and we are able to count eight points. With the La Grange Flume high above us, we cross numerous tributaries, all adding their volume to that of Stuarts Fork. Crossing the flume, we finally approach the banks of Deer Creek, the last stream to ford and the main tributary of Stuarts Fork. The trail has been rising steadily, the pitch increasing for the final climb to Cold Spring, across Deer Creek and up—mostly up, as testified to by Joe, who is reloading a spilled pack in the trail ahead of us.

The waters of Cold Spring prove very refreshing after our final effort, and the cañon walls now open to a vista of Morris Meadows with its surrounding granite cliffs and glaciated domes. An occasional stately. pine adds perspective to the view, and we can see the cedar trees of our camp-site near the head of the meadow. Whispering quaking aspens standing on a multicolored carpet of mountain flora add to the enchantment of this beauty-spot of nature.

The smell of frying bacon and the aroma of boiling coffee assail our nostrils and cause a surprising burst of speed. After satisfying the inner man, we yield to our impulse, and get busy with the fly-rod with gratifying results for our supper.

THE PROMISE OF A NEW TRAIL

Early the next morning we start for the lakes at the head of Stuarts Fork, six miles away, by following the trail from the head of Morris Meadows. On the northern slope castellated granite crags of the Salmon Alps penetrate the detritus of an overlying shale cap forming the saddle of the Hennessy Lakes Divide. Across the stream, now tumbling over a series of small cataracts, glistening domes of glaciated granite drain the melting snows of Sawtooth Mountain. We pass Portuguese Camp with its clump of pine trees and find a party of Forest Service men at breakfast. We secure their promise to start a trail from this point to the summit of the divide, separating the Stuarts Fork from Hennessy Lakes on the Salmon River side, our main objective, to be ascended later in the week.

THE UPPER LAKE OF STUARTS FORK, A GLEAMING JEWEL OF TURQUOISE AND EMERALD

After a scramble through the brush we reach the lower of the Stuarts Fork lakes with its towering crags and gigantic boulders. Relics of the activities of the La Grange Mining Company are here evident.

114

Continuing around the lake we make the ascent to the upper lake, where we find a gleaming jewel of turquoise and emerald in a setting of grotesque granite pinnacles. Patches of melting snow send their rainbow-colored spray down precipitous walls. A trout breaks the smooth surface of the lake by leaping after its prey, leaving ever-widening circles to tell its whereabouts. We assemble our rods and enjoy a day's sport with the trout-fly, completing our catch on the lower lake. We drop from an elevation of sixty-five hundred feet at the upper lake to Morris Meadows at forty-five hundred feet, arriving at camp about dusk.

CYCLOPEAN GRANITE CRAGS OF THE SALMON ALPS

After a day's rest we make for the Salmon Alps at the head of Willow Creek, a tributary of Deer Creek. The trail leaves the lower end of Morris Meadows and crosses the timbered ridge separating Deer Creek from Stuarts Fork. Following the sloping bank of Deer Creek up-stream to its junction with Willow Creek, we ascend the latter to the Bailey Mine, a quartz-gold prospect. After a short rest we climb the barren granite to the top of the divide, with an elevation of seventy-five hundred feet.

Approaching sunset casts the entire mountainscape into strong relief, making a wonderful display of its extremely rugged character. We leave our vantage-point with great reluctance to retrace our way toward camp, arriving after dark.

MYSTERIOUS HENNESSY LAKES

The trail-builders of the Forest Service advise us on the following day that the new trail to the Hennessy Lakes Divide will be cleared as far as can be done this year, bluffs of shale preventing further progress without blasting.

The more venturesome of our party start the following morning for Portuguese Camp to attempt the ascent with saddle-animals. After a short distance the trail becomes too dangerous to continue farther, and we follow our packer's suggestion to finish the climb "afoot-back."

The ever-increasing ruggedness demands our best efforts and frequent rests enable us to enjoy the view and examine the domelike structure of the burnished granite below Sawtooth Mountain on the opposite side.

Continuing, the trail disappears entirely and only an uncertain foothold is afforded by the loose shale. An occasional spire of granite penetrates the mass of detritus, forming a foreground for the glittering lakes of Stuarts Fork down below. After a boost to those of our party who show signs of weakening, we scale the rim-rock and top the divide at an elevation of eight thousand feet, bringing up against a deep snow-bank. An enchanting panorama of rugged and picturesque scenery surrounds us on all sides. The three Hennessy Lakes, unknown and unmapped, are spread at our feet. The emerald green of their waters at the shore changes to a translucent deep blue at greater depths, while an ice floe provides a contrast of dazzling white. Clumps of evergreen pines relieve the startling brightness of snow-spotted granite, with its bear-wallows filled with melted snow-water of an eery green. A peak of reddish-brown shale in the background rears itself against the distant ridges forming the valley of the Salmon River.

LAKES TO BE STOCKED WITH TROUT

There is every indication that the shores of Hennessy Lakes have never been trod by human foot until quite recently. Their waters drain into a tributary of the South Fork of the Salmon River over a cataract making access from that side very difficult, if not impossible, for man and fish; hence, no trout are found in these lakes, although the entire region abounds with game and fish. It is planned to stock these lakes as soon as the trail now started by the United States Forest Service is completed.

AN ENCHANTING PANORAMA

Following the divide we get a view of Thompson Peak with its perpetual snow and ice-field, forming a pleasing background for the upper of the Stuarts Fork lakes. We also get a glimpse of another smaller lake on a granite shelf above it, heretofore invisible.

Back of Sawtooth Mountain we can see through a filmy haze of blue the checkered outline of the upper Sacramento Valley with its prolific orchards and olive groves and fertile grain- and rice-fields.

The entire panorama of serrated granite crags, dazzling snow- and ice-fields, and translucent sapphire lakes is awe-inspiring in the extreme, and suggests to the imagination the cataclysmic forces which created this wonderland.

MAPS

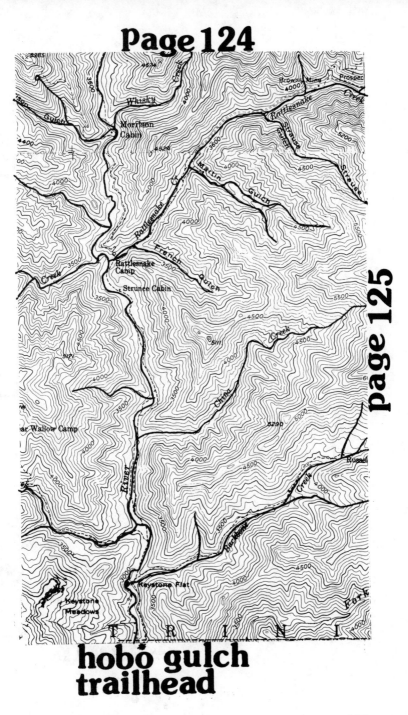

**hobo gulch
trailhead**

119

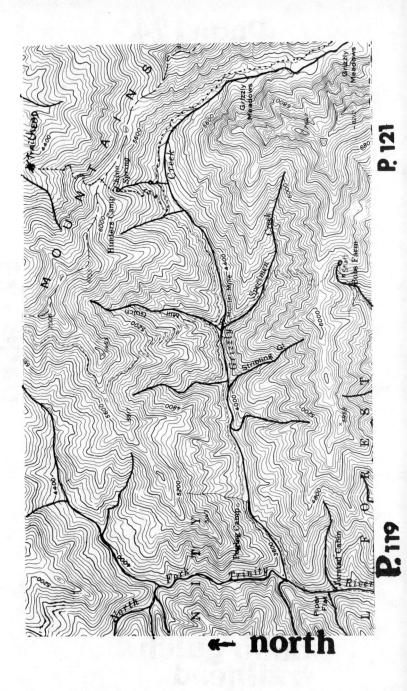

← north

120

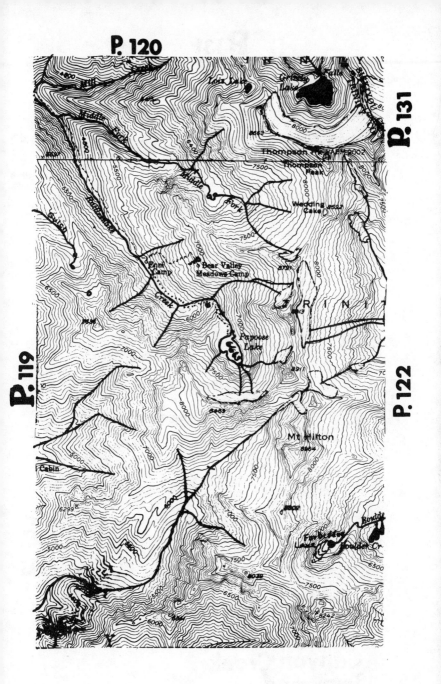

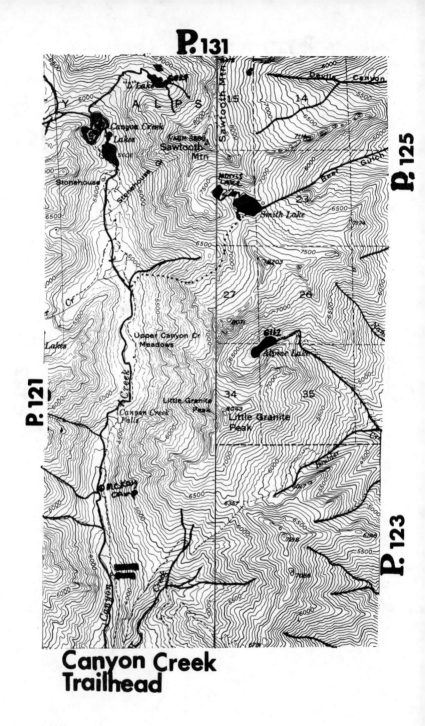

Canyon Creek
Trailhead

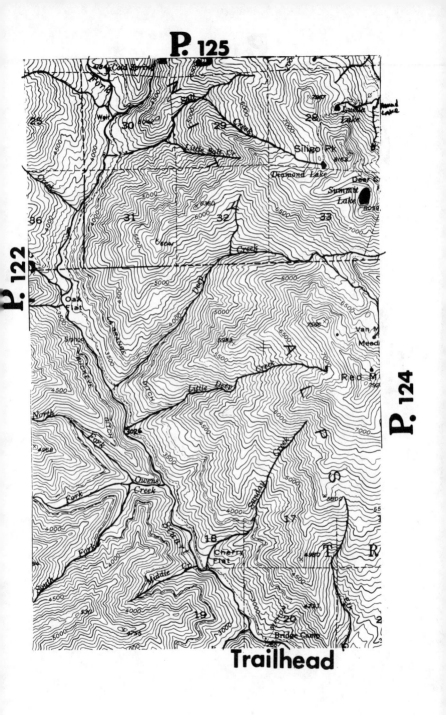

Trailhead

P. 123

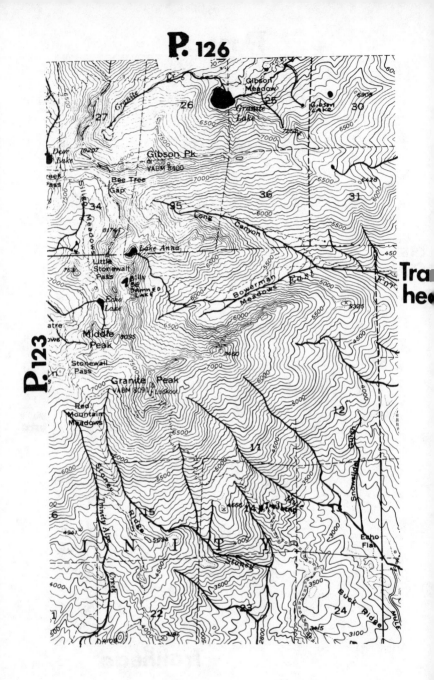

Tra
hea

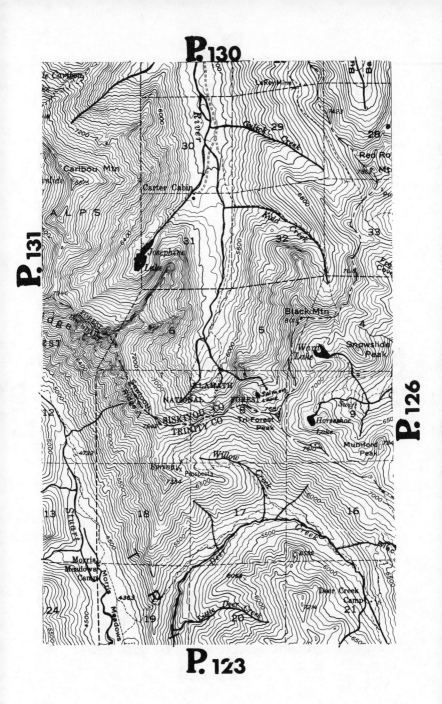

P. 129

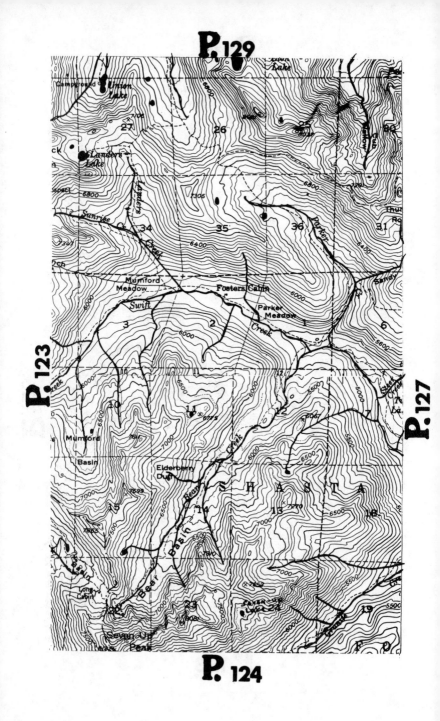

P. 123

P. 127

P. 124

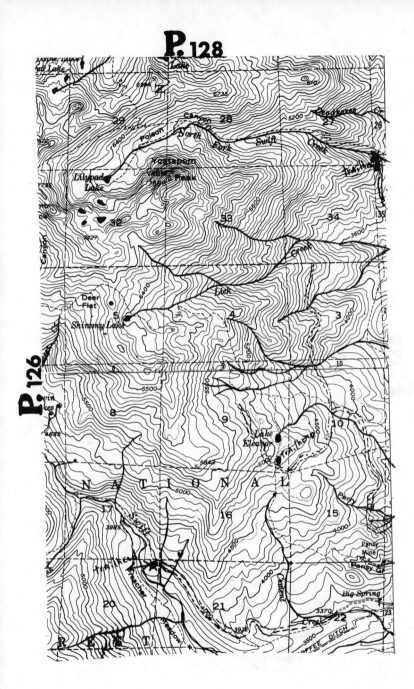

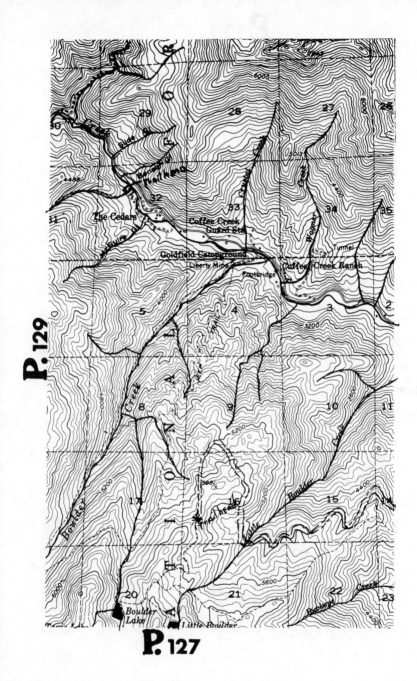

P. 129

P. 127

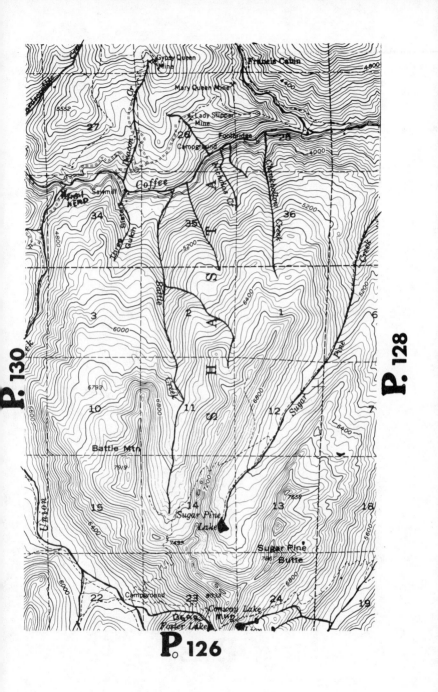

P. 130

P. 128

P. 126

129

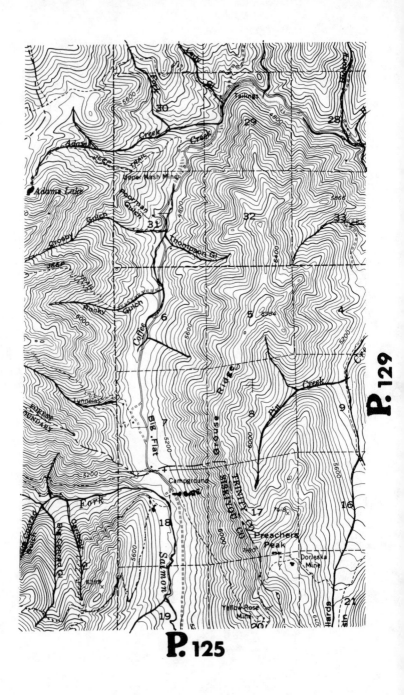

P. 129

P. 125

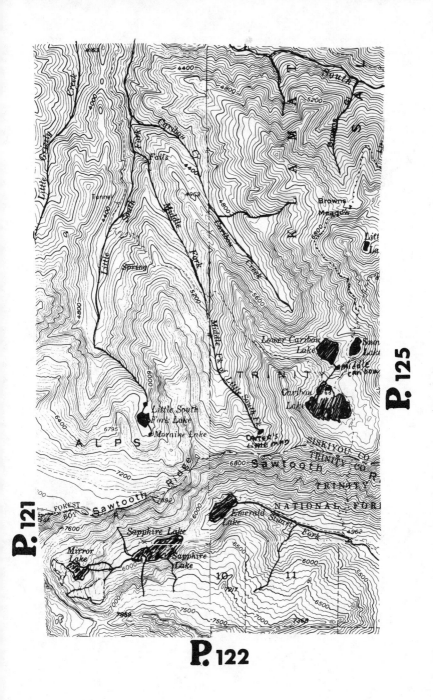

P. 125

P. 121

P. 122

131

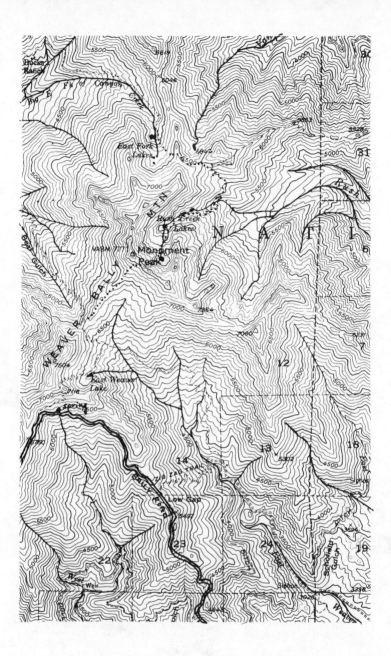